Prelude to Pleasure

Prelude to Pleasure

A Bilingual Edition
of *Víspera del gozo*

by Pedro Salinas
Translated by Noël Valis

Lewisburg
Bucknell University Press
London and Toronto: Associated University Presses

Associated University Presses
440 Forsgate Drive
Cranbury, NJ 08512

Associated University Presses
25 Sicilian Avenue
London WC1A 2QH, England

Associated University Presses
P.O. Box 338, Port Credit
Mississauga, Ontario
Canada L5G 4L8

The paper used in this publication meets the requirements
of the American National Standard for Permanence of Paper
for Printed Library Materials Z39.48-1984.

Library of Congress Cataloging-in-Publication Data

Salinas, Pedro, 1891–1951.
    [Víspera del gozo.—English and Spanish]
    Prelude to pleasure : a bilingual ed. of Víspera del gozo / by
Pedro Salinas ; translated by Noël Valis.
        p. cm.
    ISBN 0-8387-5242-X (alk. paper)
    I. Title.
PQ6635.A32V513   1993
863'.62—dc20   92-54549
                                                     CIP

Contents

Acknowledgments

My thanks to Willis Barnstone for his helpful comments and suggestions while this translation was still in the manuscript stage.

Introduction

Pedro Salinas was a great reader. This remark may seem strange—I hope to show that it isn't—because he is known first of all as a love poet of radiant and exquisite sensibility, for poetry like *La voz a ti debida* (1933; My voice because of you) and *Razón de amor* (1936; Reasons of love), and as a key figure in the Spanish vanguard aesthetic of the 1920s and 1930s. He wrote only three works of prose fiction: a novel, *La bomba increíble* (1950; The incredible bomb), a short story collection, *El desnudo impecable y otras narraciones* (1951; The impeccable nude and other narrations), and this volume, *Víspera del gozo*, or *Prelude to Pleasure*. Published during the fervor of vanguard experimentation, *Prelude to Pleasure* inaugurated a series of new narrative called the *Nova Novorum,* which appeared under the imprint of the Revista de Occidente, José Ortega y Gasset's influential publishing house. It was Ortega y Gasset who largely defined the "new art" as an elitist game of nontranscendence. That is, he saw art and literature as autonomous objects, freed from the restrictions of mimetic representation. But when he spoke about the "dehumanization of art," he left himself open to misinterpretation. Dehumanized art for Ortega meant a stylized creation, in a verbal or visual medium, divorced from the traditional aesthetic understanding that prevailed during the latter half of the nineteenth century. Ortega never rejected the "human" in art. But he did find objectionable the confusion produced when readers perceived reality and the artistic representation of reality as one and the same.

When Salinas's *Prelude to Pleasure* appeared in the summer of 1926, the slender volume, while mostly well received, came in for its share of criticism, too. The book perplexed many readers accustomed to conventional prose with clearly developed plot lines and characterizations. One such reader, curious to sample the "newest of the new," wrote in to the Madrid *Heraldo*, a daily newspaper, saying that initially she was quite disoriented. "I began to read, and the truth is I didn't understand a word of it at first" (26 August 1926). Vanguard prose was a new kind of writing and needed a new kind of reader to go along with it.

Prelude to Pleasure was also criticized for being too "French," too Proustian in style and vision. Salinas had already translated the first two volumes of Proust's masterpiece into Spanish by 1922. The influence undoubtedly exists. But there is also another pertinent connection between the two writers: their mutual passion for reading and for talking about the act of reading. Proust's eloquent introductory essay to his translation of Ruskin's *Sesame and Lilies* in 1906 is titled "On Reading." He remembers a childhood spent immersed and immured within the closed world of books. He remembers the enchantment, that glimpse of deepest truths, which for the author may come as the "Conclusion" but for the reader is but the beginning, the "Incitement" that the reading experience provokes. So he writes that "we feel quite truly that our wisdom begins where that of the author ends, and we would like to have him give us answers, while all he can do is give us desires" (p. 35).

I don't know whether Salinas was familiar with this preface by Proust, but he, too, in time came to write some of his best essays on readers and reading. Salinas was a man of great culture, yet he wore his learning lightly, even when making serious indictments of the shallowness of modern culture. Many years after the euphoria of the vanguard era, after the end of the Spanish Civil War in 1939, he reflected upon the ways people read in mid–twentieth century. And what he saw in modern readers dismayed him. He called himself the "Defender" in commentaries of a highly personal, eloquent and moving nature that would appear in 1948 as *El defensor*. A humanist, Salinas felt wrenched by the numbing effects of mass-produced modern culture, even though he was at the same time fascinated by objects like the telephone and fast cars. He found disturbing evidence of cultural loss and decay in what people read and how they read. There are now two groups of readers, he said: the *leedores* and the *lectores*. The *leedores* merely read words; they are window-shoppers of words, consuming them for personal profit. As much as Proust decried Ruskin's ideas on the utility of reading, so too did Salinas passionately hold that reading should be a disinterested act. Where is the one true reader? he despaired, labeling one part of his essay in Proustian terms, "A la recherche du liseur perdu" (In search of the lost reader). But to be a "pure reader"—those happy few *lectores*—ah, that was different. This reader reads for the sheer pleasure of savoring words, for the delight of losing oneself in a world of words. This reader is, above all, an adventurer.

Prelude to Pleasure is infused with this passion for reading and the reader. And while Salinas makes no explicit reference to the reader as adventurer, the notion is embedded in the text from the opening story, "Closed World," which begins with a train journey, to the last narration, "Livia Schubert, Incomplete," which ends with the same motif. "Closed World," as Gustavo Pérez Firmat aptly points out, is a "meditation on reading," beginning with the first sentence, "He spent two hours reading." Enclosed in the space of a train compartment, Salinas's character Andrés simultaneously undertakes a physical and a mental journey into the future and into the past. The remembrance of things past, of his lost love Alice, is clearly Proustian. But Salinas also sweeps his character into the future, through the powerful thrust and speed of the moving train, an emblem of the erotic since the ascendency of the modern middle classes in the last century. As Andrés goes to meet up with his past, to see his now-married friend Alice, he moves toward fusing past and future into one. Like all the stories in this collection, "Closed World," however, never gives us that fusion. In a word, it never ends. Everything in *Prelude to Pleasure* is always just beginning. The pleasure of this text comes from anticipation itself.

The essence of an adventure is not so much having it as imagining it, thinking about the moment. During an adventure, you can't concentrate on what it feels like. Afterward, the thing seems dulled, remote. You've finished with it. Everyone in *Prelude to Pleasure* is on the verge of something happening. There is no "non-event" in this book even though the plots are minimal, because the psychological mechanism of anticipation moves the characters and the reader into the rich zone of expectation and the accelerated imagination. As in the last lines of "Aurora in the Flesh," the pulse of life and words surges forward in the moment it is happening: "This morning's highly faithful creation and the thought itself, the figure invented and expected came crashing down all at once, because Jorge had fashioned it with what he knew, with yesterday's facts, with the past. And what he had before him, intact and brand-new in the virginal purity of paradise, holding out her hand to him, strangely without gloves, was life itself today. Aurora in the flesh."

Here too is Proustian desire. All the author can give us, Proust said, is desire. In Salinas's story, *Aurora* is just another word for a young woman, whose name spelled out is "dawn." Like the dawn, Aurora represents beginnings; and beginnings are the tiny cells of desire. There is, of course, no "Aurora in the Flesh," only the words that make her up. From the very first lines, Salinas stresses the sense of initiatory experience as the simultaneous act of reading and writing into being: "He always met Aurora in the morning, because only then is the day, freshly minted and scarcely touched, all white and expansive, like magnificent stationery on

11

which we haven't yet written more than the date." In "Seeing Her Again," the only thing the first-person narrator notices is his ex-lover's name, the letters seemingly written on every surface. And "Livia Schubert, Incomplete" begins with the sentence, "The hour of my unhappiness is written." It may appear that Salinas has simply deflected the story line onto the very modern notion of fiction as self-conscious writing. But this is only partially true. Salinas turns most of his characters into readers who interpret the reality given them—the writing itself—by turning the bits and pieces of sentences, words, and images into a composition.

All the adventures about to spurt from the point of the pen are, paradoxically, reading adventures. This swelling tempo of anticipation incites us to read *Prelude to Pleasure* as one of the most libidinized texts to come out of the vanguard period. Even in the most abstract narration of the book, "Delirium of Poplar and Cypress," the compulsion to create a composition out of the trees and other elements arises from a "delirium," that "initial desire to live." Erotic passion designs a recomposed Livia Schubert in the last story, a Livia who comes in bodily fragments of lips, hair, and eyes, and whose soul must be refashioned by the lover-narrator. Like everything else in *Prelude to Pleasure*, Livia Schubert is transformed into a verbal *objet d'art*, a prose composition. What counts is the composition.

The danger of such writing is that it fixes words too neatly on the page, immobilizing them like the sculpture of the noble—born Alfonso de Padilla, Matilde's impossible lover in "Rendezvous for Three." But even stone trembles in this strange and fabulous reality: at first we don't know what substance this waiting lover is made of. Salinas deliberately deceives us, letting us think we know reality when the truth is we don't know it at all. The poet allows us glimpses and flashes like the "loosed pack of happy hounds, a rushing throng of the sun's rays, golden, red, and tawny" that greet Matilde's arrival. And Matilde herself is metamorphosed into a modern Diana of the hunt, only to be converted back into the young lady she presumably is. But there is no such thing as ordinary reality in Salinas's poetic vision. The real shimmers, it leaps golden, mutable and disordered. It is ungovernable, the hounds of the goddess, the desired and elusive nymph, a stream of fleeing streets. The real leaves us dizzy, breathless, annulling despair like an unwanted past. Annulling memory.

This is the paradox of Salinas in *Prelude to Pleasure:* he begins with memory in a train and suddenly he says to you, Run away with it! The train speeds off with memory, converting it to desire. And desire creates an opening in what was initially a "closed world." Every character is a literary projectile hurtled into the future. It is beautifully ironic that Salinas, who later envisioned the ideal reader as an unhurried contemplative, should have created in *Prelude to Pleasure* a celebration of the modern reader as a speeding instrument of desire. But reading is no speed trap in this book. It is a sign of modernity, of the modern as ceaseless change and movement, as energy. Accelerated, reading turns into a heady experience, a subtle praise of pleasure, of the festive and the erotic in our lives. This spark, fueled by an elegant wit and humor, is all we need to set out, revitalized, on this new adventure.

On the Translation

For this translation, I have worked from the Alianza edition of *Víspera del gozo* (Madrid, 1974), which in turn reproduces the first edition (Madrid: Revista de Occidente, 1926). The text can also be found in *Narrativa completa,* edited by Soledad Salinas de Marichal (Barcelona: Barral Editores, 1976). The poet published three of the stories first in Ortega y Gasset's journal, *Revista de Occidente:* "Delirios del chopo y el ciprés" (Delirium of poplar and cypress), No. 11 (May 1924), pp. 45–51, "Entrada en Sevilla" (Arrival in Seville), No. 26 (August 1925), pp. 145–52, and "Aurora de verdad" (Aurora in the flesh), No. 34 (April 1926), pp. 1–7. The text of "Delirios . . ." is identical to that of the original edition, except for one punctuation change and the spacing between paragraphs. "Entrada en Sevilla" contains only a few minor variations in paragraphing, punctuation, and two slight lexical changes. The same kinds of small variations are found in "Aurora de verdad."

To my knowledge, only two of the stories—"Delirios del chopo y el ciprés" and "Volverla a ver"—have appeared in English, as "Ravings Anent the Poplar and the Cypress," translated by Victor Llona, in *The European Caravan,* edited by Samuel Putnam et al. (New York: Brewer, Warren, and Putnam, 1931), pp. 402–5, and "Reunion," translated by Marquise d'Elbée and Eugene Jolas, in *Transition,* No. 4 (July 1927), pp. 40–45. An Italian translation of *Víspera del gozo* by Cesare Greppi, titled *Vigilia del piacere,* was published in 1976 (Torino: Einaudi).

Translating *Víspera del gozo* was a sheer delight. Not that I didn't knock my head against the wall in frustration when I couldn't find the phrase, the word, the tone, or rhythm to try to match, or at least approximate, Salinas's verbal wizardry. But working this closely with the text breeds a sense of awe at the breathtaking craftsmanship of Salinas's style and vision. As Robert Spires notes in *Transparent Simulacra* (p. 130), *Vispera del gozo* is "arguably the best achievement in Spanish prose fiction of a work clearly identified with the . . . [vanguard] movement."

Further Reading

The poetry of Pedro Salinas (1891–1951) spans three decades, from *Presagios* (Presages) in 1923 to the posthumously published *Confianza, poemas inéditos* (Confidence, unpublished poems) in 1955. Some translations exist: *Lost Angel and Other Poems* (a selection of *Todo más claro*, 1938), *Truth of Two and Other Poems* (selections from *La voz a ti debida* and *Razón de amor*, 1940), *Zero* (*Cero*, 1947), *Sea of San Juan: A Contemplation* (*El contemplado*, 1950), English versions by Eleanor L. Turnbull; *To Live in Pronouns (Selected Love Poems)*, translated by Edith Helman and Norma Farber (1974); and *My Voice Because of You* (*La voz a ti debida*), translated by Willis Barnstone (1976).

None of Salinas's many essays—on reading, Rubén Darío, Jorge Manrique, twentieth-century Spanish literature, etc.—is available in English, with the exception of *Reality and the Poet in Spanish Poetry* (translated by Edith Fishtine Helman, 1940). Of his prose fiction, neither *La bomba increíble* nor *El desnudo impecable y otras narraciones* has appeared in English translation.

For those who would like to know more about Salinas, John Crispin's introductory study, *Pedro Salinas* (New York: Twayne, 1974), is a good place to start, as are the lovely pages the great Spanish poet, Jorge Guillén, wrote about his friend in the introduction to *Reality and the Poet in Spanish Poetry* (1940; Baltimore: Johns Hopkins Press, 1966). A detailed biography, *Pedro Salinas and his Circumstance*, by Jean Cross Newman appeared in 1983 (San Juan, P.R.: Inter-American University Press of Puerto Rico). José Ortega y Gasset's *The Dehumanization of Art* (translated by Helene Weyl; 1968; Princeton: Princeton University Press, 1972) continues to be the indispensable point of departure for understanding vanguard art. Highly recommended as well are Gustavo Pérez Firmat's *Idle Fictions. The Hispanic Vanguard Novel, 1926–1934* (Durham, N.C.: Duke University Press, 1982) and Robert C. Spires' *Transparent Simulacra. Spanish Fiction, 1902–1926* (Columbia: University of Missouri Press, 1988). Finally, for the Proustian connection, see the French writer's exquisite essay, *On Reading* (translated and edited by Jean Autret and William Burford; New York: The Macmillan Company, 1971).

For the Reader

The day Ulysses stepped into the public library was a momentous day. Ulysses wandered all over the place, in great amazement. Other than Hades, he had never been in such cramped and bulging rooms before. He also wasn't quite sure why he was here. Of all his adventures this certainly was the strangest one. Not a thing stirred. He heard nothing, only a dry, ancient cough now and then, or the crackled shuffling of a page. No enchantments here. Not a single warrior, goddess, or cyclops. In fact, every eye he saw wasn't fixed on him, it was fixed on a series of black and white tracks, an endless trail that stopped in a pool of white and resumed, mysteriously, at the next turning. Baffled, he picked up a book. The librarian, a kind soul who viewed herself as a guide for the perplexed, came over and pointed to the title: *Prelude to Pleasure.*

"This book, sir, is for two weeks only. It's new, you see, and there's a waiting list."

Ulysses sighed.

"I don't think I'll ever learn to read," he said, "but I sure would like to know what they're saying in there."

Now the librarian, who remembered even the books she read when she was nine years old, remembered that line of dialogue like it was yesterday.

"Why, you're Ulysses Macauley, and you said that when you were a little boy on page 203 of *The Human Comedy* by William Saroyan."

Only this Ulysses was a grown man, a little torn at the edges by experience maybe, but still eager for adventures and further from Ithaca than ever before.

"Just try this book, sir," she said, with a special pleading look that for a moment held the gleam of an elusive nymph, the startled flash of white feet fleeing as he raced in hot pursuit.

"Ah my dear, I have you now," he thought. "You are in your true shape, and this is why I am in this strange place."

"Tell me the story," he said.

"Well, that's just it, sir. There is no story."

"No story?"

19

"No. But you're in it. In fact, you're the main character."

Enormously pleased, Ulysses picked up the book again and leafed through it, wondering if he would recognize himself somewhere in the dense maze of tiny tracks.

"But where am I?" he asked, bewildered.

"There," she pointed with one slender prophetic finger. "You're there in all those words. The story is all those words. You make up the adventures as you go along."

"You mean *I* tell the story? But isn't there a poet in the house?" he asked, desperately.

"Of course there's a poet, but Mr. Salinas is a very modest man. He doesn't like to take all the credit. And he likes you. He really does. That's why you're in every scene, every sentence, every letter of the book. Besides, he figured you have so much experience in this business of enchantments, he could use a man of your background. You know, spells, transformations, quick changes."

At this point Ulysses was thoroughly confused. He didn't know where he was or even who he was. "But if I'm in every scene, how can I be the poet, too? I mean, what does Mr. Salinas take me for?"

"Oh sir," enthused the nymph of the library. "Mr. Salinas is your best fan. He thinks you're simply delightful. And he's given you the biggest part of all."

"Oh? What's that?" Ulysses asked, glowing with intense satisfaction by now.

"Why, the Reader of course."

N.V.

Prelude to Pleasure

Closed World

He spent two hours reading. Next to him, on the seat, the book was closed. A book with large print, wide margins, a complicated, appealing plot, one of those books we buy on a winter's day, expecting to read it that night by the fire, but then, a few lines later, we realize it was written for another time and place; for a bright afternoon of travel—only then will it give us that delicious sense of pleasure as if it were squeezed out of an orange. But then it often happens that during the trip for which it was meant we come across a fine-talking fellow traveler and pass the entire time chatting, while the book lies abandoned, its cover an unheard yellow incessant scream, like a rejected virgin lying among the pillows. And so it happened this time, because the two hours reading were spent without a book in front of him, looking through the train window—and the thing read was impossible to catalogue as a literary genre. Andrés was reading a new landscape, an unknown country. Of course the reading wasn't being done the way he would have liked, because he couldn't turn the pages, that mission being carried out, at a rough, uneven clip, by the engineer. But no doubt because he was new to the line, the engineer completely ignored the extraordinary beauty flashed in the ragged rhythms. A page would come, for example, that was tender, moving, as classic in its simplicity as a Homeric farewell, written in crystalline sentences by the curve of the river, seeded throughout with groves and verdant blooms like well-placed epithets, two or three superb images, bright pure clouds crowning the period. But then the train would swiftly turn the page at ninety kilometers per hour, with scarcely time to read it through, let alone learn by heart and carry inside the way he wanted once he'd leafed through it. On the other hand, five minutes later the train would make a short stop at a third-rate station, like a page of print in which a sidetrack—shabby freight cars with paint peeling, a gray depot wall in the background, and a sign bearing the word *Lampmaker*—made up an astonishing and unquestionably real "slice of life." But it was so miserable and insignificant that you couldn't figure out how it could have come from the same author, and you

23

suspected it was an apocryphal insertion. Or take that little stream descending like a cascade visibly promising in the distance a burst of tumbling, free-flowing rhythms. As soon as the train came alongside, the engineer, under the pretext that they were crossing the bridge, unleashed a metallic clamor calculated to drown by drought the liquid grace of the water. Another time he cut off the wonderfully delicate trill of a bird, miraculously saved from the noise of the speeding train and exquisitely initiated like the *rites de passage* of adolescence, with a brutally shrill whistle. This seemed to serve no other purpose than to propagate in the romantic souls of young ladies from a nearby fourth-rate capital the twice-weekly idealized vision of a luxury train, the four o'clock express, which like chain links—from engine to caboose— connected two great cities. And then, something ill-timed and fatal like those sudden distractions that assault us in the middle of reading without knowing where they come from, as if an inner breath of air propelled them, thrusts between our concentration and the printed word a strange and impenetrable ingredient: unexpectedly, the locomotive would throw out here, toward our side and aided by the wind—coming from outside this time— billows of thick gray smoke, behind which perhaps the most exhilarating scene of the book was vertiginously fleeing, hopelessly expiring before our eyes. Even worse was that time when a sketch of a steep gorge, cragged and pearly-hued, was unfolding at the peak of its glory, and suddenly the story stopped dead in its tracks, as the small windowpane turned illegible, black with the gloomy blackness of a tunnel inside a tunnel. That really tired him out; it offended his sense of dignity as a rich and idle dilettante reading and taking his pleasure whenever he liked. So ignoring the train whistle that invited him, as he emerged from the tunnel, to resume once more his haphazard reading, he picked up his bag and removed two bulky address books.

For some time now he had been in the habit of recording the names and addresses of his friends—like double entry bookkeeping—in two notebooks. In the one were annotated alphabetically the last names, the way everyone does. But in the second notebook the heading of each page corresponded to a city, which included right after it a list of all the acquaintances he knew there. Andrés, extraordinarily keen on cities and characters, at once timid and curious, but equally fond of company and intimate solitude, had discovered the perfect mechanism in this system of interdependent notebooks. It was thanks to the nearly always fortuitous and irregular meshing of these two cogged wheels that he might decide one day to take the Indies mail train and the next, the Orient express. The new, the unknown, all that was tremulously desired and distant, such cities, jotted down in the second notebook, only took on movement and life thanks to the rotations that the known, the familiar, the names in the first notebook would stamp upon them. To meet people, to know that a friend had changed his address, was for him a broadening of possible worlds. His life was being mapped out in a form of geographical-sentimental cartography, complete and without lacunae, where there weren't any uncharted lands, where every city, no matter how enormous and remote it was, had its explanation, its port of entry in a name, in a human being, in the memory of a love affair or a friendship. Say he hadn't visited such and such a place celebrated in history and in art, didn't know a soul there. But one day, an old schoolmate announced his transfer to another diplomatic post. That's all he needed to go off in conquest of the immense city, with no more weapons than a few directions indicated in a small book. Yet he was as confident as the multimillionaire fondling the miniscule steel key that will enable him to open, easily and painlessly, the enormous door to his storehouse of treasures. Another time, in a hotel he met a woman who was born and raised in an unimportant city of a historic nation, a city that until then had appeared to him like an inaccessible and coveted island captured in one of those primitives' paintings, already outside time and with no ship to take him there. And suddenly, that distant point was within reach of his desires, in a kind of silken magic just like the swan of *Lohengrin,* all because a very pale young lady with waving, minute gestures like feathers said to him one afternoon: "Why don't you come and spend a few days? I'll show you around." From that instant, the fifty thousand souls attributed by the census, until then asleep in a long enchantment, awoke and returned to their mosaic of daily tasks, wearing the look of people who will be watching us walk by very soon with a friend by our side. And when he wrote in the second notebook the two names—the city, his friend—joined together as in those cards for newlyweds, a particular place in the world lost its air of apprehension, the veiled reserve and vague warnings, as though the offer had coincided with the glittering inauguration of a rail line, constructed fifty years ago and used by countless trains now.

He looked at the name of the city to which he was headed: Icosia. A minor European capital, with an elegant charm, timid and quiet, like the charm of a famous beauty's little sister, less handsome, less intelligent, but who nevertheless always possesses a smiling, happy face, a lesser expression all her own. Next to Icosia he had written and then erased something, like an abandoned hope and, then, with very recent handwriting: Lady Gurney. He smiled. Because the truth was he didn't know this particular friend, this Lady Gurney who had smoothed the way to Icosia. He found himself flirting with this reality, caressing it fearlessly, like an unloaded, expensive revolver, perfectly harmless. "I don't really know Lady Gurney. I have a lot of photos of her, it's that mania of having her picture taken all the time. Like that lovely one with the evening dress she wore to the Trinity dance, the only one made against her wishes, simply because I asked her for it. But the best one of all is where we're standing together, the day of the Oxford-Cambridge regatta, the day she kissed me. Incomparable. It has a line from Swinburne written on the back, I forget which one. . . . It's amusing to think that I don't actually know Lady Gurney." And he threw the contradiction into the air, making it fly like cigarette smoke blown by his breath into the close, warm atmosphere of the compartment, following it voluptuously, though invisible, with his sight. What would Lady Gurney be like? Those brown eyes—but would they be that color now? That walk of hers, quick, energetic, and perhaps overtaken by now, through some mysterious and remote rhythm only she perceived, by a rare and languorous *ritardando*. And that smile she had—dry, intermittent, without mystery perhaps, widened, expressive and deep, fixed forever on her face, available at any moment, with no need to stalk it—was it the same? That evocation of Lady Gurney provoked a sudden uneasiness in him. And just as you tear away from the loved and familiar face the silken mask behind which she was talking and flirting with you a moment ago, to find another person, a stranger, so he threw out the window the new and conjugal name of Lady Gurney, which had only existed for six weeks, and found behind it, throbbing and trembling, Alice Chesterfield, the unmarried Lady Gurney, offering him their own friendship in her faithful arms. It was useless to continue deceiving himself: the notebook spoke the strict truth, Alice Chesterfield written below and then erased, and to the side, Lady Gurney. He would have to take reality, sharp and painful as the steel point of a pen, and pierce his heart, like scratching out the text of a notebook. He would be scratching out two years of his life, in London, Cambridge, Ramsgate, two years of . . .

"The gentleman is staying at Icosia Beach or the city?"

The train attendant's question, abrupt and disjointed, like scissors cutting his inner monologue, left him mutilated, splitting in two the best and most delicious part, the part that remained within, the unexpressed memory.

"In the city."

That was where Alice's new husband, Lord Gurney, lived, that was where his married friend had lived for barely two weeks. And like one of those exchanged wedding gifts, Alice and her husband had offered him Icosia, this small fruit, once very high up and hanging from an inaccessible branch, the branch that Lord and Lady Gurney now grasped bringing it close to the ground, so that their friend could effortlessly take the fruit ripened by so many nostalgically remembered springs. It seemed to Andrés that he could already feel a deliciously new taste in his mouth, the juice of Icosia. Precisely then the words entered through the train window—wild and fluttering like those gulls skimming the earth telling us that the sea is very near even if we do not see it yet—heraldic, annunciatory words written on large billboards: "Icosia, 10 Kilometers," "Omnium Bazaar. This Week Only: Linens," "Pears Soap Pears Soap Pears Soap," "Icosia, 5 Kilometers." And then, signless, anonymous and self-evident, but piecemeal, because it couldn't fit in whole, the city itself. They passed in between two long rows of wagons, those miserable, third-class wagons full of goods that pile up afternoons on both sides of the itinerary indicated by official proclamation. Like the idle people of a great city awaiting the arrival of a foreign potentate, they would see the Vienna Express come in proud, impetuous and brilliant. The main station was already coming out to greet him with a gesture of welcome, gray and electric, displayed in arc lamps, reflections dancing over the rails, officious offers from the porters. A few people were waiting. Andrés searched among them for the figure of Alice. And that only because the force of habit was such that he had completely forgotten she was married. His eyes, clumsily, routinely looked for a single silhouette instead of the couple who ought to be waiting for him. But he didn't find anything or anybody. He stepped out of the compartment. And suddenly, there on the platform he saw a letter waiting for him. How had he recognized it? The envelope didn't have Alice's familiar round, delicate handwriting on it, but a strange and angular pen. Nevertheless, he was convinced that the tall, serious manservant holding the letter in his hand and thus completing his inquiring gesture, was looking for him. So it was.

"This letter is from Lord Gurney. The car is waiting for the gentleman outside." He didn't want to read it right there. "Let's go." As he left the station, he saw nothing, not even the petite and voluptuous avenue, enveloped in flowering acacia, like that look with which a woman or a city invites us to follow her, to go a little further. Everything in him was sliding toward his hand, weighing and testing the sealed letter, stiff and oppressive, undoubtedly with something tremendous inside. Once in the car he opened it: ". . . Alice died the day before yesterday. I will wait for you here,

27

in the country. . . ." Icosia, at the first touch of his lips and scarcely bitten into, gave back the most bitter taste of all, the taste of mortal earth. He uprooted it from his mouth, hurled it out the window to the green valley below, where it lay shining, like a rotting and deceitful piece of fruit; because the automobile, without having penetrated the city, having scarcely even nibbled at it, was already racing toward the country, turning its back upon the cypresses' curved farewells in the cemetery on the hill.

Arrival in Seville

They left at six o'clock in the afternoon, when the sun from the
street was by then a little worn out. Morning steel had subdued
it after vain and stubborn attempts to enter reticent domestic
interiors. As it was a May sun, quickened by its own fires, it
dreamed of stretching out in the shadows, in a patio, a bedroom,
in any of those shaded places that offered an excellent defense
against the sun's own heat, and where one ought to feel right at
home, without the sun. It tried out everything, candles, locks,
hallways, windows. Everything impenetrable. The golden patio
awnings, the massive doors ajar, and the stiff, white blinds of bal-
conies and belvederes resisting like heroic virgins. If once it
slipped furtively past an unattended and very high, small window,
there was bad luck attached. Because then it would fall upon the
smooth, hostile surface of a mirror, only to bounce off, wounded
by its own sharp edges multiplied in glints and reflections, and
thus battered and abused, drag itself along the walls, fleeing from
its own image. And then it had to stay all day in a sunny street,
the blond leonine mane hanging sad and limp on the ground.
Forgotten and indifferent by now, it didn't even feel the shadows
advancing with the stealthy step of the melodramatic villain,
sharpening the cold fist of twilight.

Claudio went down the stairs, and crossed the patio, with its
freshness, the sound of water, its charm sustained miraculously as
in baroque architecture, in the pulsating, crystalline curve of a
fountain. To exit there was a low, dark front door, but as the outer
light was more promising and more sharply defined than the
light in the patio, Claudio did not experience that slightly sad,
shrinking sensation we feel whenever we go out. On the contrary,
it seemed to him he was going into something; and the truth is,
of course, he was going to enter the coveted city, Seville. But at that
moment what he saw beyond the vestibule wasn't the landscape of
a city but the powerful form of a waiting automobile that blotted
out everything else. Closer up Claudio saw that on the other side
of the car, and scarcely leaving space for a person to pass, rose
the facade of the neighboring house. The automobile was so close

to the door that the first step Claudio took in Seville was not supported by the soft Andalusian ground, but by a neutral zone of distant nationality, the car running board. "Gentlemen do not touch the ground here," Robledo said, with a knowing smile. And while she covered herself with the thin blanket, Claudio, twisting his head about, looked at the facade of the unknown house they were leaving. When they arrived there some hours before, it was night, so that despite having been happily settled in, he still hadn't seen it. He looked at it now the way one looks at a person we know very well, from the inside, because she wrote us countless letters or because someone talked about her all the time. Seeing her for the first time, he searched eagerly for signs of corroboration or disillusionment in her face. But the house—attractive, reserved—said nothing to him. The white facade, now in shadow, was dull and sunless. The two balconies, the shutters, were like a popular song, with a kind of simple happiness painted green on the iron bars, but the blinds, starched and stiff, corrected the impression with a dry scholarly interpretation. On the roof railing there were flowers, quite enormous blue and white flowers, but they were scentless still lifes, safe from any contretemps or danger, in season or out of reason, without a spring or a summer, painted, dry and brilliant, and set in ornate leftover pottery. Everything about the house gave the appearance of last night's joy and love, delicious and hard to explain. Suddenly the car started up, leaving all that behind. The house became whiteness streaked with green, and then it quickly disappeared, easily, falling behind, out of sight and memory like an island or a remembrance that sinks without a trace of the pleasure or place that once existed. "Pay attention now, this is Seville," Robledo said.

The car, narrowly enclosed by houses to the right and left, began its heroic journey. The street, immobile but possessed by the dramatic dizzying speed of the car, began to unfold forms, lines, thousand-hued changing spaces, broken up and then instantly brought together, completely incoherent; with the same speed and skill the sleight-of-hand man demonstrates the brightly colored objects used for his game, not so much for the public to see them than with the malicious intent in mind of creating with their flashing sequence a confused image, suitable for any kind of spectator fraud. Yes, of course, probably when all this quieted down, out of this confusion of colors Seville was going to emerge, clear and whole, an offering in the palm of someone's expert hand, on the Guadalquivir flatland. But for the moment you couldn't see city or streets, not even its individual parts, the houses. The only thing the eyes caught were fragments, bits and pieces of walls, rose-colored, green and blue walls, and from time to

30

time, like a rounded black period trying to give an appearance of order to chaotic prose, a doorway into which your gaze always plunged too late. You scarcely reached the wrought-iron gate and wondered through which of those geometrical passages you entered to get to the suspected patio, when something else started all over again, leaving that behind: a colored wall, the edge of an abrupt corner, an iron railing almost always closed, but that once revealed, with heartrending haste, the tender melting, uninhabited light like a captive gazelle behind bars, of a room lived in, a room someone had just left to which he would return any moment now, someone you will never see. Suddenly, at a crossing, the street they were driving on swerved, turned to the right, escaped waving and brightly colored like a flight of gypsies. But no: your eyes were mistaken. That fleeing street was another one and not yours, another one that started out from there and fused with this one, the same and yet deliciously distinct. That was why his heart kept thinking he'd lost it, doubting yet deluded as on that morning he followed the sister of the woman he loved for a few moments, for the remote likeness of their silhouettes.

From time to time he glanced up: a headlong rush of twisted belvederes, unfocused balconies, secretive and vacant, paraded by; and higher up, the sky, a blue patch, slight and soft, glimpsed between borders of geraniums and carnations, threading its way among the flowerpots on the roofs, a narrow little path through which you would have to walk single-file. Even so it was impossible to pass now, because right in the middle a leaden, motionless cumulus cloud, with nothing to do, had fallen asleep. For Claudio the conventional Seville of panoramic vistas was disappearing, a distant definition in the landscape with two lines—cluster of houses, the Giralda tower—cutting across one another in a strictly geometrical ideal. Remote, the city itself could not be defined, thus purified and particular; it simply existed, close to you, very complex, always shying away from the straight line, pleasing like the body of a ballerina with subtle breaks and sinuosities. Its intentions changed direction constantly, and by virtue of not wanting anything continuous, of ceaseless permutations, demonstrated a powerful will, at heart rectilinear. Thus overpowered, a man at no moment went where he intended to go, but where the caprice of the city, its willful, indomitable soul, might lure him, for pleasure or pain—exquisite dilemma—with such attractive peripatetic possibilities. Impossible to remain undecided here in these streets, silken and penetrating like nocturnal whisperings. But impossible, then, to go anywhere by following the rules of the road, to achieve a design as though you were involved in some rational undertaking superior to the city's complicated norms. You had to go

31

through Seville, loose and easy, as though you were floating in the invisible water of a dried riverbed, walk without purpose, wanting to move on but without ever arriving, pulled along by those water-less currents in an automobile adrift like a zigged gondola without its zag. But where indeed was Seville? Surely it was through those veins, those pink and blue veins, which weren't veins at all, but Andalusian streets—Aromo, Lirio, Escarpín—that one reached its secret and difficult heart. Every new vision was the ultimate adventure, the last enchantment, and yet, for every vision another one next to it was immediately substituted, the same way a note from a string flies from its place of birth, because in the per-former's fingers there is already another one waiting to overtake and complete it. The imagination had to join together a particular section of white-washed wall, that hallway over there, an ironwork gate, using not your own perspective—that had already slipped away—but the view from the house next door. Then, above all that, you put in the other balconies and terraces, added a visible but conventional sky, and you'd reconstructed ideally what in truth didn't fit into the view because of the narrowness of the street and the rapid pace. That was why the city, which seemed so real, trembled like a phantasmagoria, in imminent danger that all those fragments, which in reality were perfectly united, might not hold together, arbitrarily assembled as they were in the imagina-tion, and that everything would come tumbling down, in a crudely painted, fake earthquake like the ones they show with rhymed comments on fair banners. He was seeing Seville, yet he still had to continue imagining it. Even deep inside it, the city was for him something uncertain and elusive like the woman you loved, a product of real details, but scattered and nebulous, even if unified by the lucid fantasy that coordinates them in a higher en-chantment.

He felt like looking more closely, getting out of the car. But at the same moment he was going to say so, during an abrupt swerve of the car, Robledo's traveling bag fell to the floor and the contents spilled out. Robledo and Claudio bent over at the same time to pick up the things scattered about. It took a while, they had to remove the blanket, grope in the corners and, when their hands touched for a moment, he saw the color in Robledo's pale face rise, saw her become embarrassed, then go white again, blush of blushes. After this episode, Claudio, who hadn't forgotten or lost sight of the dislocated, vividly colored street, found, as though it were the last thing lost on the car floor, his desire to get out; and he said, still bent over: "Listen, why don't we walk around a bit here?" "Why here?" Robledo asked. "This is pretty awful." Sitting up now, he looked around: it really was pretty awful. In the two minutes their search lasted, the gaily colored houses, the streets, Seville, everything marvelous he'd glimpsed had disappeared, like the last delightful trick to vanish into the conjurer's magic hat. And now they were in a wide street, of modern design, with tall gray houses, and in the distance the countryside, the end of Seville. Claudio's astonishment, his dejection, it seemed, were going to remain unexpressed, when suddenly the car horn, communicating by some mysterious conduit with his heart, uttered a harsh, lamenting roar, made to seem like a warning to the uninitiated pedestrian, but in which one recognized very clearly, now as before, the centuries-old despair, impotent and magnificent, with which the mocked Pan sees how once again the desired and elusive nymph escapes him.

Rendezvous for Three

When Angel entered the church it was only a quarter of six but the clock was already striking six o'clock; because the city possessed (and this was its most secret charm, the reason why life here was so relaxed and generous) a careless and aristocratic way of counting time. He was used to living in places where this inexhaustible yet elusive wealth, perfectly coined in diverse kinds of monies—hours, minutes, and seconds—was scrupulously measured out and administered, piece by piece, by clocks and traffic, by human labor and municipal lighting. Thus there could never be any error in the reckoning, and every creature received his exact share of sixty minutes, odiously identical, on the hour, every hour. Without understanding that there were people—all those lucky people—who needed much more, you lived by the lavish and accelerated rhythm of happiness, freed from the servitude of the *how* and the *how much;* you spent the hour recklessly, on anything at all, on passing fancies, kisses or laziness, squandering it in a few minutes and so immediately ending up empty-handed, without a thing. All the while, those unfortunate people whose vital signs were minimal, who were content with very little, were standing there in front of you, passing back and forth between their bloodless fingers those golden leftover minutes, counting them one by one, without knowing what to do with so much money, because they had nothing to spend it on. They were like those terribly rich Americans who promenade forlornly through great hotels, propped up by the crutches of extravagance and philanthropy, wealth without purpose. But here, in Sarracín, there was nothing of that: time was naked and behaved in a liberal and amusing fashion, as in a Bacchic festival when the body loosens corset and suspenders, garters and clasps, everything that fits it oppressively, rigidly, and reveals itself free and easy, rosy, leaving no doubt of its complete surrender. The hours expanded, exquisite and unexpected; they arrived before arriving the way the person we are anxiously awaiting arrives long before he is here, his silhouette alone preceding him, as it slides toward us on the slippery surface of that bridge we construct over distance, halfway

34

between his smile and ours, separate yet united. And the same thing when we leave, when we already thought the hours definitely gone, they returned, under any pretext, a pretended forgetfulness, disguising the desire to stay a while longer with us. So in that city at around a quarter of six it was already beginning to strike six o'clock.

That was what the San Esteban clock said. Because it towered over the tallest houses, the clock dominated large stretches of the horizon and could see, before anyone else, the clouds, the trains, and the hours from far off, as soon as they peered around the bluish edge of time. And even though they were very remote, glimpsed with difficulty through fog or night, the clock saw them unerringly, without ever confusing the high, solitary eagle's flight of one o'clock with the sensual and arrow-swift couple, like inseparable tower storks, of two o'clock in the afternoon, and certainly not with that happy flock, mischievous and free-falling, of twelve o'clock, which appeared around midday, leaping and jumping like children who've escaped from the classroom, those apprentices of tables for dividing time in some celestial tony school. Six o'clock was, then, the first of San Esteban's hours to appear at the top of its tower, in clusters, fresh and reddish like early cherries, a jubilant sign of premature pleasures. Six o'clock was for all those who were expecting something, for those who were in a hurry to live. They could hear this clock better than anyone else, and they would say: "It's six o'clock already," knowing it wasn't true. Abandoning everything they had begun and could have finished in ten more minutes, they left leaping down the stairs, in happy haste, as if they were going to arrive late, supremely aware of the delusion, but deluded anyway. It seemed to them they had opened a shortcut in time, a shortcut to avoid the long and painful turnings of the real six o'clock, taking them swiftly and secretly to the same place: where she, the one waited for, would not yet be, because she knew perfectly well the clock was ten minutes fast.

Then starting with those first strokes of the bell, the same hour was striking in different clocks, identically and deliciously transformed as if some whimsical celestial fingers were amusing themselves by playing improvised variations on a well-known popular theme, alternating between the raised white piano keys of the city's rooftops and the black keys of those sharp streets in shadow. It was all done so cleverly that anyone with a tin ear sometimes didn't recognize the first motif, because of the skill with which the performer changed the rhythm and tone; so that now uncertain, the listener wondered what time it really was. The hours, then, even though they came from the high bell towers, didn't fall sparkling like firecrackers over mere mortals but crept up playfully,

35

having already arrived but not arrived, smiling with the antici-
pated smile of promised possession, distant yet, perhaps inacces-
sible, as in the most practiced and delightful of flirtations. And
for one who was afraid of a certain hour of the day, for the timid
soul waiting for that hour to land suddenly in his heart, thanks
to those small and inoffensive harbinger clouds announcing the
arrival of the disastrous black cloud, the hour of truth, there was
always time to take refuge in distraction itself, in invented, artifi-
cial noise where neither time nor memory could be heard.

And then six o'clock arrived, the six genuine and legitimate
fair daughters of the meridian hour. But having been previously
announced by the royal issuance of so many bastard, look-alike
sisters, all of them very noisy, the six now arrived wrapped in the
most august dignity as befitting royal personages, and no doubt
to distinguish themselves from the others, in silence—because six
o'clock sharp didn't ring, didn't chime from any clock. The only
one to function punctually, without ever miscalculating, marking
the hours with its hands, was the courthouse clock, mute and bell-
less, the perfect model of a nearly divine justice that never errs
and is carried out in secret. Thus the right hour was there, but
reticent; it existed somewhere in a resonant void, pure and with-
out guile, like those truths that are perhaps the most exact thing
about us, but precisely for that reason cannot be modulated into
sounds. They spend their life like medieval princesses, there in
the high castles of their gaze, hope in their eyes, or elusive and
enclosed within the inner rooms of the heart. No one, then, heard
the true hour except as between two approximations, a little be-
fore or a little afterward. But it was already here, and everyone
who had waited for it, because he had a rendezvous with six
o'clock, at six, embraced the hour, fresh and trembling, in his
arms, hurrying the kisses a little because you knew you couldn't
be very long at it, no more than an hour kissing. And yet it wasn't
always so. There were clocks that, doubtless, because they were
embedded in ancient towers of the eleventh century, had that
deep, slow movement of the Romanesque, and invariably lost time,
ladened with nostalgia, unwilling to separate themselves from the
past. With these clocks it turned out that at seven six o'clock still
hadn't finished. The hour in some parish churches lasted five, even
ten minutes longer, an exquisite and unexpected prolongation,
resembling that quarter-hour of delay the train always brings
when a friend is going away. They were well-stolen and well-
guarded minutes, a theft against time who, like Cronus, will never
recover the son who got away.

But six o'clock, slow and tardy, floated lazily in the liquid and
transparent air like the debris of the shipwreck of time. Angel

clung desperately to this last resort, anxious not to sink altogether into that most profound of certainties, cold and black like the bottom of the sea, that Matilde would not be coming.

"It's barely six," he'd say, "she could still come." Even though he knew that six o'clock had been there for ten minutes, the way death, stealthy and certain, is at our side the last fifteen days of our life. Yet we play the innocent, dissimulating, pretending not to notice, bustling and bubbling with projects as if somehow we could escape it. But faith by inference wasn't enough. He knew only too well that it was a delusion, that someone had to tell him so, that someone else and not him had to make good his expectations. Unfortunately he was alone. The personages sculpted in stone on the pillars had the secular habit of silence. If anyone did speak, the words issued from his lips as scraps of engraven scripture, a mute phrase in Latin, abstract and despairing of the world, like a divine standard raised in silence. He walked over to a corner of the bishop's chapel. A shell exquisitely carved in the soft roseate stone of Hontoria radiated the warm flesh tones of a human ear. In a low voice he said:

"She could still come, it's barely six." And now he heard it, he heard it very well, enraptured by his own word. Narcissus without water but with lover. That hope that persisted within him emerged from its pure limbo and assumed a body in sound, transformed into matter by the strength of illusion. Thus audibly animated, it advanced toward him, his and yet not his, offering his very heart's desire as though it were an astonishing gift. But there are voices, and this was one of them, with a double echo: one from without, heard in the rocks and the walls, which faithful and true repeats voices just the way we wanted them, and another surreptitious, inner and strange, which we didn't count on, and which deforms our words and returns them sounding like the very opposite of what they were saying. And then it is we understand that the word from outside, the one we gave to the air and from which it returns, is a false thing, an empty and hollow lie, while the truth illuminates silently, revealing itself to us in that inner echo, unexpected and unprecedented. So his "she could still come" bouncing off the cave walls of the heart sounded maddening to him: "She isn't going to come, she isn't going to come, she isn't going to come." Then he let go hope, let it drop like a smoldering half-burned piece of wood, marvelous to see from afar, but now when he went to pick it up, burned his fingers. Better said, he exchanged it for another: maybe he had been mistaken about the hour, and she was going to come exactly one hour later, at seven. Nevertheless he was sure that Matilde had said six o'clock. She was like a princess who plunges her hand into a small bag of pearls and chooses from among the twenty-four hours of the day that iridescent but unpolished hour of six o'clock. It was, Angel remembered, as though that number suddenly served to explain the world to him, that world which a moment before, when he did not know if he would be able to see her or not, seemed like an insoluble and confusing problem. The limpid sky, running between two rows of trees like a river, carried along like floating, lily-white legends, one, two, three, four, five, six, precisely six little summer clouds, toward an unknown sea. A six would surely win the great twilight game of roulette, there in the horizon's red square where the sun like a ball was going to drop, hazy and unshining. Even the life that ran bluish and winding through Matilde's bare arm tried out on the ivory-white base of her skin with fine veined writing, a botched six, incorrect but unmistakable. No, he hadn't been wrong. The time for their rendezvous was six, and she wouldn't be coming at all.

But in the end, what did it matter? Because the funny thing was that this meeting, which he had looked forward to since yesterday, wasn't with him. If Matilde had agreed to come to the cathedral at six o'clock it was to see Alfonso de Padilla. The day before, Matilde had been talking with her friends in the university cloisters, and they all praised the young man to the skies: his hair long and curly like that of a page, the exploits attributed to him, his noble appearance, that cool yet melancholy gaze of his, worthy of a knight of old. The best time to see him was at six, in the cathedral. And then Matilde, who had listened in silence, said firmly, looking straight at Angel: "Tomorrow, at six, I'll go to the cathedral." Angel had wormed his way into the sweet, juicy fruit of that hour, like a greedy maggot ready to devour it completely, for he meant to leave nothing at all to the other mouth to whom it had been offered. What did it matter if it wasn't for him? At any rate he would see Matilde. He would be stretched out on the edge of the rendezvous, lying on the shore of six, the way one is on the bank of a river that doesn't flow for us, that surges toward something else. Yet we seize in passing, as though on the sly but without touching, exquisite delights, simply by seeing it race toward the sea. That was why he was wandering alone through the enormous cathedral.

Well not exactly alone, because Alfonso de Padilla could be found in the church well before Angel came in. But his appearance certainly surprised him. In his right hand he held an open book, but unread, with one of those empty, useless gestures that persist, leftover even after the soul and the will to act have departed, leaving behind a space impossible to fill with the gesture itself. A space just like that soft, very white hollow lingering in the afternoon air when doves have passed over. From the book flowed the sadness of a perch without its bird, for the gaze that a moment before rested on it, double, black and pointed like claws, escaped now, on an unknown flight. The hawk was off hunting, no doubt, something well-concealed, because the searching look was not aimed outside himself but turned toward the inner recesses of the youth, after an invisible prey. Probably to pass the time he had lain down, nearly stretched out on the stone, resting his cheek on his hand with such an elegant disdain for everything around him, that when the sexton passed by he made out as if he didn't see him, intimidated by his hauteur, and as if he were long accustomed to such disrespectful lounging about in a holy place. But the most astonishing thing of all was that he didn't even attempt to chase away that dog, stretched across the stone and asleep, with a fleecy white coat that in the twilight gave off strange marble reflections. There he was lying faithful and emblematic, at the feet of Alfonso de Padilla.

It was now almost seven o'clock. The sexton with clinking keys in hand began pursuing the last light of day, dawdling behind in the side chapels of the church. As soon as they heard him, the last frightened glimmers, afraid of remaining closed up all night, there in the dark, escaped, leaping through the high narrow window and leaving the church in shadow. Angel moved toward the exit slowly, painfully burdened with a dead hope. But suddenly the curtain belonging to the door in the back of the church was lifted: like a loosed pack of happy hounds, a rushing throng of the sun's rays, golden, red, and tawny, came in, all of them howling and leaping around the brightly lit and handsome figure of a woman, blond and slim, carrying underneath her arm a quiver that looked like a small parasol. The trees glimpsed for an instant outside in the distance before the door closed were no longer humble municipal acacias, the little garden in the cathedral square. They had been transformed by the feminine figure, to which they served as a momentary background, into a dense woodland of Argolis through which the huntress Diana, ardent and virginal, ran, completely puzzled at having come across in its midst this strange and boldly proportioned construction, a Gothic cathedral. The sexton spotted her immediately as a pagan goddess, and terrified by her audacity, flung out as his only defense the professional anathema: "We're closing, we're closing!" accompanied by a great clanging of keys. Now the curtain had once more fallen, and with it the hounds of the goddess, her golden escort of twilight, disappeared. Diana stood still, without a sound, without a voice, without a soul, before a new age. And then, perverse and feminine, with her divine power, in a clever non-Ovidian

39

metamorphosis she took on the respectful and timid appearance of a young lady who has come late to the cathedral, the very figure, the exact features of Matilde. Angel came up to her.

"I'm very late, aren't I? What a pity. I won't be able to see him."

They left together, pursued, ejected as from a frustrated paradise, by the keys and footsteps of the sexton. But Angel felt a secret, satanic pleasure, because he was leaving with Matilde, walking by her side, in flesh and blood, on this pulsating, pure afternoon, while his gorgeous hated rival, Alfonso de Padilla, lord of Olmos Albos and page of Queen Isabella, having met death in a frontier ballad, before the Plain of Granada, would lie shut up in the church, in the shadow of a flowery canopy of stone, in his Gothic grave, the rendezvous for three now ended.

Delirium of Poplar and Cypress

To Mercedes and María Salvador, remembered among their poplars of Burgos.

Introduction. Traveling by train, gazing idly, his thoughts on vacation, he lit upon those two trees planted at the deepest bend of the horizon, solitary and the same, one as like the other as the two handles of an immense frustrated H. The mind, half-asleep and inattentive, was jolted awake, and piqued by childish haste and zeal, launched into its duties, left the train, scaled steep slopes, made shortcuts shorter, leaped over gullies, and by now in the far horizon, became convinced by the mounting evidence of sight and touch that the two identical trees were a poplar and a cypress. His mind returned hurriedly to the next station where the train remained waiting; and seated in the eloquent solitude of his compartment, perfectly balanced by the fleeting and allusive company of lateral landscapes, he wrote in his American notebook: "Aphorism for tomorrow; from a distance, the same; close up, so parallel that they will never meet." His writing came out shaky, perhaps from the emotion coming from the discovery or from the swaying seat that any rolling convoy confers upon the most confident aphorist.

Poplar. Last night, under the arched murmuring of the stars, you were, confess it, content with your fate and even diverted for a few hours of profound, purified immobility. But at the first light the morning wind leaps, and once again you throw yourself into the tantalizing trial and error of profiles moving over still horizons, of silhouettes losing their outline in that initial desire to live; everything full, overflowing, the form you assumed one minute ago overwhelmed by the rush of so many forms into your heart that now want to try themselves out. You invent yourself over a hundred times, only to undo what you invent a hundred more. You exist like a chain, from the link before to the link afterward. Your standing is low in the neighborhood, and with that frantic handwaving of yours, poor poplar, you'll never be more than a sower of intentions in this strong-willed Castilian plain that knows

41

how things should be done. He won't leave you alone for one minute, that sly and slippery angel who whispers in your tiny ear the dangerous information that your form will only take shape in the agonizing succession of infinite deformations.

Cypress. No one saw you training, your apprenticeship was so short. A well-aimed root, barely thrust into the earth, already exuding the sap of subterranean discipline. With the exalted stateliness of the achieved form, all your efforts in life are concentrated in insisting, fiercely confident, on a straight profile projected against soft blue landscapes or tormented, jagged skies. And when the day comes it finds you, and when the night comes it finds you, hard at work, patiently sculpting yourself, eager for the singular advice of your own shadow spilled on the ground night and day.

Poplar, water. Every landscape dances to the sound made by water, sea, river, stream. But in the summer, with oceans far away, riverbeds dried up, mountains without snow, where is the water of Castile's life if not in this moist ceaseless movement of poplars, in the vast wave of poplar groves in the distance, in that seething shudder of foliage, and in that dry drop, the leaf of the poplar, with which the breezy afternoon spatters us? And illusory rivers and seas make their waters dance behind this transparent yet exact mask that a dry Castilian dusk affixes over the landscape.

Incidental anecdote. We had spent eight days roaming the asphalt meadows of the city as our only countryside, and only the luminous shadows of the street lamps, with their marvelous nightly leafage, gave us repose. And since you were feeling nostalgic for the earth and poplars of Castile, I took you to the museum. You didn't touch earth there either, only polished wood, the kind whose oil of turpentine stirred in you vague images of strange fields of grass with an artificial penetrating perfume, in the Australian outback. You didn't see sky; instead, expert glasswork where the lights of hot-spirited days are tempered and tamed. And no horizon other than four walls pockmarked by the peepholes of paintings, on some of which they had forgotten to put the glass and you could lean over into the subject, the body half in, half out. I took you to the portrait gallery, and there, in the dark eyes of an unknown personage (black suit, limp beard, earth tones) was your tree of Castile, timid and vacillating soul, loving and weepy like the summer poplar just rained upon, all ashake before every little thing, light, air, smoke, poplar. You wrote as a joke, in the catalogue: "This picture of an unknown gentleman identified as by El Greco is a portrait of a poplar, vaguely attired, anatomy uncertain. See landscape gallery."

Poplar, autumn. The quiver of silver, fervor of gold, May pomp, October pride, good-bye! The winter wind digs its spurs into pain-

42

ful penitence, and by the roads of Castile naked poplars twist and turn with the dry clicking of stripped skeletons, flagellating their white bones, the ultimate misery. On the ground, lust in its agony, the dry golden leaves scatter in fear, driven mad by persecution and torment, pursued by the harsh hounds of the north wind.

Cypress, facing death. Cypress stands for an irrevocable decision to save itself. Not for one single day did that determination, materialized in the attenuated thrust of an unbreakable silhouette, desert its celestial post. It wore the same set of rough clothes, threadbare and gray from the rain, scorching sun, gale winds and years, the kind that offers the best deal in divestment. This is when, on a night filled with mist, like death, like the border with death, this is when we see the cypress, bones splintered and spindled, that long, incorporeal whiteness like the configurations in paintings meant to represent souls, lightly held by the hands of two angels as they ascend to a well-deserved heaven.

Poplar, wood for a cross. If you do not die for us all, you certainly suffer for us all. No one, neither the cloud in the leaden sky, nor the bloodhound asleep in his rough bed, nor the flyaway curls lying still on the napes of young girls, nor the bellflowers submerged in the bullrushes, no one senses the enemy, that subtle little wind passing through the air. No one shudders, no one sacrifices himself. With your infinitely tiny leaves, with you only, poplar, does it collide. And while the whole cowardly afternoon, dull and unmoved, shrinks from anxiety, you desperately defend as everybody's sentinel, in an apparent dead calm, your duty to feel anguish delicately.

Aurora in the Flesh

He always met Aurora in the morning, because only then is the day, freshly minted and scarcely touched, all white and expansive, like magnificent stationery on which we haven't yet written more than the date. Four sheets of paper into which we can pour all the jumbled, passionate outbursts of the heart without having to squeeze in the writing except a little bit at the end, when night falls and there is never enough space. As the time fixed upon was ten o'clock, naturally Jorge woke up at half past eight. The first thing he found, there by his side, enormous and impalpable, was Aurora's absence. Absence that, for a moment, seemed inexplicable, since his lover had been with him all night, and more responsive and affectionate than ever before. There was no reason now, precisely when he opened his eyes, for him to stop seeing her, for that conversation, barely initiated on a fascinating subject (but impossible to remember now that he was awake) to remain poised and tantalizing, like tracings preserved in an incompleted palimpsest. He jumped out of the narrow single bed and went straight to the desk, with that mania of his for recording everything, to put down the first adverse event of the day: "8:30, lost Aurora." But as he sat facing the diary, before he could pick up his pen, the last sentence written the night before leaped out before his eyes: "10:00 tomorrow, meet Aurora." The morning he'd dreamed about last night was, he discovered, already there and ripe for the picking, like a plum on its branch, hanging from the trees in the square and swaying calmly in the air; that morning was now. With the knowledge he felt serene once again. And Aurora, like one of those objects that fall from our hands but that we succeed in catching just before it hits the floor, reappeared without ever having been lost. He opened the balcony windows, looked at his watch, in search of corroboration. Between the dreamlike, talkative Aurora who had just left his bed and the other real but silent Aurora whom he was going to meet very soon in the museum, flowed ninety minutes, one

44

hour and a half like sluggish waters between two twin yet separate river banks.

But Jorge didn't stop to stare sadly upon that still distant and desired shore. Instead, he bathed, got dressed and had breakfast, that is, he worked happily and profitably on eliminating the sense of separation. By half past nine he was in the street. And although the rendezvous with Aurora was for a half-hour later, as soon as he came to the boulevard he was already running into her. Not that he found Aurora suddenly, all at once, or that she unexpectedly materialized before his very eyes. No, it came little by little, advancing slowly, the way the philosopher happens upon truth, by laying the inner groundwork based on accurate, real data. The first thing he saw on the asphalt ground was the shadow of a petite dressmaker passing by, a shadow exactly like Aurora's, when the two of them were going through the park the other day. Jorge bent over to pick up her fan, which she had dropped, and there behind her in the golden sand he stumbled upon an exact and epitomized likeness of Aurora, blue and vaguely deformed like an image seen in the bottom of a pond. He had barely walked out into the street and already he found Aurora's shadow imprinted on someone else's as though it were her own. And right after that, at every step he kept coming upon more things of hers. Because even though she was unique and unmistakable, she seemed to be everywhere, flowing like a precious yet wasted fluid, water without a form. Take that tall dried prune who was crossing the square at that moment. She was wearing a little straw hat from Italy just like the one Aurora had brought back from her last trip to Florence and put on one day blushing like a romantic tourist. Jorge continued on his way, quite content at having flushed out in such a short time two fragments of his love, of a perfect whole: a shadow and that trifle of straw. Suddenly, on the platform of a passing streetcar that was spattering everyone with drops of attention and clanging bells, there went a girl—her face invisible, turned toward the other side. To keep her balance she'd taken on a position of twisted calm, of agonized stasis, just like the pose Aurora tried out one afternoon on the ship, over the turbulent waters of the Canal, when she wanted to suggest the idea of a particularly exquisite and difficult line of a sculpture seen in Strasbourg. A little further on, he saw a young woman who, despite her honest appearance, was wearing as if it were hers, Aurora's décolletage, hanging from her neck like a precious cloth pendant, triangular and rose-colored. And from a street running into the boulevard, reaching at him sideways through a series of associations came the soft distant undulations of the Mediterranean, pierced by the wind, as if Aurora, who was constantly changing clothes, had thrown into the sea last night that delicate little blue blouse that trembled at every breath, that little blouse of hers.

Little by little the distant and still invisible figure was taking shape out of the scattered and confused coincidence of all those diverse external elements the city had to offer. But, thanks to the original model, to the exemplary image he wore engraved in his heart, he was able to arrange each element in its place like the pieces of a puzzle. Very few were missing now, because the city was wide-open and intensely alive, plunging deeply into sea and mountain, bursting in trade and extraordinarily abundant in races and varieties of clothing, forms, lines, colors of all kinds flowing over him: pieces coming at him, still and perfumed like the fruit, the glitter of jewels and the sheen of fabrics behind shop windows or vertiginous and vague as a stream of dresses, the faces of Arab officials crossing at top speed in an automobile, or fragments of unhappiness tied and tormented by the thought of release in the green gestures of trees behind park railings, and the luckiest bits of all, free and ownerless, vagabonds in the morning air, shreds of clouds, kites. And yet, such rich resources aside, no matter how clearly he saw the desired original in his heart, Jorge couldn't really have Aurora complete and of a piece until she was standing there before him. He would always be missing certain essential things, empty spaces he couldn't fill until she gave him, with her first words of greeting, in the simple form of "Hello," those three unique and irreplaceable pieces: the way she looked at him, her smile, and her voice.

He was now drawing near the museum, carrying with him that fragmented figure, a delightful, incomplete little statue to which he still had to give eyes, draw lips and pour in speech, to make her a living and perfect work of art, something he couldn't achieve without Aurora's collaboration, an easy, painless collaboration at that: merely her presence. He went up the museum steps and, as always, the doorman called out to tell him he had forgotten to leave his walking stick. It was very early and the only public in sight were those insignificant and lesser personages of Dutch portraits who spend the whole day, immobile and admiring, watched over by the museum guards (after all, who can you trust these days?), so they can see close up and in great detail so many solemn and stuffy princes and gentlemen painted by Titian and Rubens. Aurora and Jorge had agreed to meet every day in a different gallery, following a strictly chronological order. This, on the face of it, had the disadvantage of seeming pedantic and academic, but it gave Aurora a mutable and exquisite backdrop for advancing more and more toward light and color. Thus she would pass through delicate transitions, from the rocky settings, plain and dry, of Giotto to the flowers of Renoir, from a theatrical, solemn conception of the world in the Venetian manner to that gay, tempting and half-naked liberality of landscapes filled with nymphs, painted ten years ago.

They had been seeing each other for nearly a month, and that day they were to meet in the Turner gallery. Aurora would be the only living being inhabiting that nonearthly paradise, Eve created in reverse, before man and waiting for him in a world recently invented, still blurred, smoking and trembling, with a splendid Italian pine as the tree of knowledge. He pushed in the heavy door and immediately felt the dense, warm atmosphere, the ninety-five degrees, of the painting. Eve, Aurora, wasn't there, creation had been postponed; and Jorge began to stroll through that grandly elemental cosmos, where air, water, and earth were not yet differentiated clearly one from the other because God had just separated them, yielding to Aurora's desire, to the first, Adamic whim of woman. Indifferent now to the paintings around him, he returned to his imagination, where he saw her, almost complete, adorned from top to toe in those intangible garments glimpsed on the way and in his memory. Yes, that was it: she was really coming, but she was so familiar now, there inside him, so like the real thing, practically invented by him, that her actual appearance wouldn't surprise him at all. It would seem like that last and most felicitous inspiration that completes a poem one has worked on for a long time and now knows almost by heart. He went over to the wide balcony that looked out upon the docks. Precisely at that instant the fleeting image of a feminine figure slipped from the visual field he dominated and turned, making as though to enter the museum. Yet that elusive splash of color with the straw hat, the blue bodice, and rosy décolletage corresponded to the inner image of Aurora traced by Jorge over her real image of the evening before. Yes, it had to be her. But while Jorge was having his last doubts about the ephemeral and lost silhouette, Aurora, without his realizing it, had entered the room. "I'm a little late, aren't I?" The words reverberated above those deserted landscapes, reaching Jorge amplified, prolonged by the echo they generated in a "Rocks at Dawn" that was hanging to his left. He turned, and when he saw her, an immense astonishment overwhelmed him: Aurora was wearing a dark little chamois hat, a gray suit with no décolletage at all, and she was coming toward him alone, without yesterday's blue-tinted shadow, without her street shadow from a moment ago. This morning's highly faithful creation and the thought itself, the figure invented and expected came crashing down all at once, because Jorge had fashioned it with what he knew, with yesterday's facts, with the past. And what he had before him, intact and brand-new, in the virginal purity of paradise, holding out her hand to him, strangely without gloves, was life itself today. Aurora in the flesh.

Seeing Her Again

As I looked out from the hotel balcony, ushering in the light of day, I might have seen the huddle of houses and the port, the earth that sustained me, the sea that brought me to her, and very far away, the concealed line cloaking the coast of Europe, where I came from and where I was born. And yet from this balcony that faced a thin line of white woods, the cresting waves, the sea-green undulations of pine groves, work and leisure, God and man, practically a perfect philosophical and autobiographical synthesis of my twenty-three years, the first thing I saw, the only thing I saw was her name. It had rained the night before, so that it was clear, legible, brilliant like a decision made by an uncluttered mind. "The letters," I calculated, "must be at least twenty meters high, because from here, and I'm far away, I can read them easily." Reveling sensually in them, I cast my eyes over the enormous characters, relating them with a delightful sense of satisfaction to the person of flesh and blood I knew. The *L*, firm and precise, like her profile set in motion, and now immobile. The *X* with its two intersections, just like those two contradictory caprices of hers that crisscrossed one afternoon; like something she wanted at first and then didn't because then she wanted the thing she'd given up for it. I saw very clearly that she really wanted both of them that way, joined in conflict, as in the letter. The *S* similar to her jokes, sinuous and stroked to a finish with refined perfection, but at times so dry, so disturbing they seemed more like a series of *Z*'s. I drew away as quickly as I could from the *B*, fleeing from its sight, from the entangling double intimations of a firm and briefly eternalized breast, breath suspended. The *Y* saturated me completely, like dew, with the memory of an afternoon tennis game when her enigmatic character, supported by a graceful body, maintained itself, stretched and taut, on the white point of her foot, as if she were walking on some invisible cord extended between afternoon and night over the reddish abyss of dusk. But on no letter did I dwell more than on that discreet sign of her heart, a delicious, hieratic *V*, offering me the purest and most desirable good, like a sterling spirit who stands on the rooftop all day looking up at the sky. When skimming clouds played hide-and-seek with the sun, here light there shadow, they descended upon the *V* in simulated, luminous contractions and expansions of the heart, galvanized into an intoxicating but false life. It seemed then as if my blood was beating to the time marked by that inhuman, optical pulse. Even though I had meticulously closed off the name, gone outside it now, and taken leave, it was still her name. And I still remembered the last embraces, the final good-bye, finished and well-rounded with which at the same time as she moved away from me, she was already extending the loose end of memory. My eyes grew tired from staring so much at the name traced in gigantic black letters over the red roof of the great ware-house on the wharf. I had to stop thinking about it.

Just then, as if my desire for something else yet the same had been understood, a ship entered the harbor, delicately suspended from pale blue theater flies by a tenuous thread of smoke, so light and nearly invisible that it appeared as if the ship were moving by itself. Wanting distraction I picked up the binoculars, brought the steamship closer into view, and cast my eye on the name of the ship. And oh God! The same letters peacefully sunning them-selves on the rooftop and indelibly stamped onto the constant shadow of my thoughts were now flaunting themselves, painted completely white like a yachtswoman's summer outfits on the sides of that spectral steamship. The waves darted in hastily, bowing in foamy ecstasy, one after the other, like glib and repetitious compliments before a pretty woman. And there was no doubt in my mind that the retinue of sea gulls swooping insistently over the ship was biding its time, waiting for the right moment to fall upon those letters and carry away every one of them in their beaks, the precious treasure scattered forever, like diamonds senselessly separated from the perfect jewel by clumsy thieves. As the name majestically entered the bay, two or three sirens waved ragged handkerchiefs in welcome. A tugboat officiously rushed to meet it, playing out the role of the proper servant who meets the car and lays out the running board where his lady's foot is going to alight. Then the name made some turns, came to a stop. Only the slight rocking in the harbor, the sea's last flirtatious waves before the calm, in grateful memory of the crossing, kept the name from being as legible and still as the one on the rooftop. I was about to put away the binoculars when I saw a brightly colored pennant fluttering from the topmast in the breeze, with some-thing trembling, written on it. No, it wasn't her name. Too large, too many letters, to get them so high up. No one thinks we'll get to heaven wearing the clothes and jewels that in this life we couldn't do without, but rather stripped and synthesized into pure soul. Thus written into the blue skies of morning she rose to the top after her name had first been distilled into two initials, P.B., incomplete yet essential, and the white pennant proclaimed with two red letters her final triumph, the taking of heaven itself.

But what an exquisite delight this, to turn your back on the soul in order to see it, having to open your eyes wide like a vigilante of reality, instead of closing them gloomily, in search of inner visions. To remember her it wasn't necessary to touch subtle mental springs and let loose a flood of secret images. Merely the purest exercise of your senses or the sweep of your eyes over earth, sea and sky were enough, knowing you'd find her anywhere, happy, the nape of her neck tickled by the wind in the pennant, calm and idle on the rooftop, and still trembling and streaked wet in pale reflections, when the white letters painted on the sides of the ship reappeared duplicated but distorted in the bay water. Every spot on earth, the furrowed spaces hollowed out by a keel, a plant or a bird's wings, were stamped with her sign. They were singers of the power and the glory of one creature over the world. And suddenly, when I brought the focus in closer to the wide boulevard lying at my feet, I saw that an enormous gray truck was carrying off at top speed, with the happy roar of an abducting bull, her name painted in blue. The name would go through the city and the countryside so that astonished eyes could spell it out rapidly without understanding its significance, like a fleeting sacred scripture. She would be exhibited, like the banner of a conquistador, proud and indifferent in the town he'd just won. By now I was so worn out by her overwhelming presence I closed my eyes, so I wouldn't have to think about her. But she was also here by my side, inside me, written backwards like a page copied from a mirror, which at first we don't see clearly but which we understand immediately as soon as it is read the other way round, beginning with the left side of the heart.

I decided to amuse myself, trying to escape her. I read a while, went to the bookstores, bought writing paper of different kinds choosing very carefully, stopped in front of a billboard, reading attentively the announcements of some repulsive spectacle. In a word, I composed an artificial and false hour, heartlessly, the way one composes out of mere caprice and distraction a little poem in Latin, which somehow turns out to be an acrostic. Without meaning to, we begin each line with one of those letters engraved in our minds in a set order, the very letters we wanted to forget with such a *divertimento*. Desperate I returned to the hotel, crept into the elevator, my room, the bed. Suddenly the sound of the telephone jerked at the silence, ringing it like a broad bell.

"There's someone asking for you here."

"Who is it? Did they give a name?"

And with my eyes shut, the way a prisoner closes them before the rifles of the firing squad that is going to take his life, in order not to see the inevitable, the inescapable facts, I waited for that name to rise, spoken, sung, exalted upwards to the fifth floor by the doorman's harsh voice, that name—*Miss Priscilla Beexley*—which went straight to where it already resided, my heart.

Very unlike myself, I decided to use the elevator. It was incredibly slow. It simply wasn't coming, maybe it would never come, maybe the bell I had just pressed was out of order and I was going to stand there on the landing, twenty-five meters from Miss Beexley, cut off from her forever, suspended in the unclaimed limbo space of a stairway landing, between heaven and earth, like an angel punished by God. Because obviously I couldn't even think of the other route, of going down step by step until I reached her. That was the way one usually went to all the unimportant things, like museums, the club, the pier, Europe, America, the unknown. But at the present moment I was not heading for a place identifiable as north or south, as caprice or despair, but somewhere with access only by sudden and decisive immersion, by a fall so imperative and yet at the same time, so self-willed that the force of gravity pulling at us seems like a free and easy exercise, a graceful function of the human. My mind was so set on one thing that I couldn't find the strength to move my body, because every ounce of energy went into wanting, a kind of paralyzed wanting. And so the stairs were out of the question. Where I was going you had to go in blind, silent and stiff the way Egyptian mummies walk, solemn and perfumed, in precisely the opposite direction, into the temporary tomb of the elevator. And even *walk, go,* are not the right words. It was more like a sponge sinking, which as it descends goes faster and faster because the fall itself, the water, the weight, saturate it with an accelerated sense of urgency in falling. So I would sink until I'd reached fine sand strewn with the most fragile, complex hours like pieces of coral, with intricate and vaguely defined blooms, species of algae no one has ever cataloged, shells closed or half-open, deliciously iridescent, not a single pearl in any of them. Sand that slept under the cape of time. Because where I was going was to the past, Priscilla's and my past. After three years, I was going to see her again for the first time.

Sudden, silent, and lit like a flame, the elevator jumped in front of me, revealing a heart paid by the hour. I had only to take one step inside. And life began to run vertiginously in reverse. Time was coming apart, as the elevator passed through it. As I went past each floor I could read as though it were the scale of a thermometer the distances being wiped out. The three years that separated me from Priscilla at the beginning were only two at the second floor, scarcely a few months as I crossed before the polished door of the mezzanine, and were reduced miraculously to weeks, days, hours, with a speed exactly parallel to the elevator's, as we headed for the ground floor. And now downstairs, when the servant lifted the curtain hanging before the door of the lounge where Priscilla was waiting, I discovered that the three years of living in absentia were now completely unlived and that this day of seeing her again was the perfect abolition of time-in-between, all traces of it having been deleted. It was the very day we had parted.

Livia Schubert, Incomplete

The hour of my unhappiness is written. Not a minute before nor a minute after: precisely at 1:35 tonight I am going to be miserable. In the Middle Ages fortunes and misfortunes were written with a quill on smooth, celestial parchment, trimmed with suns and rain and crows in capricious flight who decided, as the wind blows, a man's destiny. Nowadays, it is much simpler: fate, at least my fate, is within easy reach. It comes printed in huge press runs of an ordinary book, and can be found in the alphabetical index, dizzily running down the scale of names and numbers, the way you run down a keyboard in search of a note—which one? do, re, fa?—with your fingertips and sustained here, in the flesh, your heart. Here it is: page 223. Lovely page, superb literature evoking gorgeous, unknown lands in a penetrating, plain style, without a single adjective, a style so hungry for precision that it exhausts all verbal possibilities, leaping from letters to numbers and expressing itself as a superior poetry, in the figures of mathematics. Nothing superfluous here, not a particle, not a rhyme. Prose or poetry? Who knows. Words came naked and pure, well-arranged, right on target, one after another as in lines of poetry, similar from a distance to verses or to waves, each one different yet related to the next one, and all moving toward the same thing. And then, to the right and the left, like two identical and very firm borders of land, from two and two make four, numbers, double margins of numbers seeing the immutable, the eternal pass, as though they were two rows of poplars and in between flowed that singing stream of runaway words. This entire strange composition is blocked out in black and bears the title of a very modern poem: "Itinerary, 63." My unhappiness is written, not in that enormous and hard-to-consult book of destiny, but in a train schedule, in the line that reads: "Lucentum, arrival, 1:32; departure, 1:35." My misfortune doesn't bear one of those pompous and definitive names that people like to give: grief, despair, disillusionment, death. It is called, simply, the Paris-Prague Express, Number 22; all sharp and metallic, like an arrow shot electrically by the taut bow of the Gare du Nord, which will fall somewhere in Prague,

Walisova, without having encountered another obstacle in its path except for this unexpected soft heart of mine. There I stand in its midst, ready to be pierced cleanly, bloodlessly, tonight at 1:35, when it streaks through the sky of Lucentum and carries away wrapped in sheets, my Livia Schubert, rocking her like a child half-asleep, with the sound of iron, so that she won't remember me and will fall asleep quickly. In the end it doesn't matter that my unhappiness will be punctual, made precise in time, separating a life from life in a moment as mathematically foreseen and inexorable as executing the death penalty. None of those childhood uncertainties, that time when the end of the world was announced, scientifically guaranteed, for such and such a week, and which cost me so many sleepless nights and a cruel disillusionment and this incurable skepticism. No, this time disaster will come at the appointed hour. Already it must be lining up to make its appearance, a brilliant one, with the restaurant tables all set and the fire prepared, its strength gathered up in order to thrust every last inch forward, wholeheartedly, with its enormous weight, as soon as the stationmaster's whistle, round, tender and short like a child's finger, sets it off. And now, at six o'clock, the same hour when I will see Livia for the last time, in ten minutes, that black cloud will start off, all sails crowding through the night air, five hundred kilometers away, that black cloud that will have to discharge its flash of lightning among us at 1:35, opening in the earth an abyss so enormous in distance that we end up, she on one side, I on the other, separated for the rest of our lives.

I say good-bye while she is thrust in that sleep of six o'clock in the afternoon, that short and galloping sleep going at full tilt like a one-thousand–meter Grand Prix. I look at her for the last time, I look at myself in her for the last time. Because this interweaving of the two of us, Lucentum, summer, her lips, the day and the hour of our meeting, her laughter and my unhappiness, this living together, joined one to the other for the space of two months, all of this is going to come apart as soon as Livia, with her very slight voice, filed even thinner in farewell, cuts, inevitably and unintentionally, the string of beads holding us together. I see myself now, day after day, bent over looking for them, scattered on the floor, fumbling at every instant, thinking that the afternoon, crystalline and transparent like a diamond, that I see ahead of me turning the corner at twelve o'clock, is an afternoon spent together, that this busy city of three hundred thousand people continues to be inhabited when in reality its population, Livia Schubert and her spirit, have emigrated. She went far away, two thousand kilometers, like a persecuted queen, to found a new kingdom and populate it with joy and smiles, raising her invincible and gaily colored banner above the mist.

Right now I am still in Livia; I am still something in her: I am the disorder of her sleeping body. Her hair that trails golden, like a long shadow at dusk; her right cheek, pale and lifeless, contrasting with the other (I was at her left), glowing and flushed; that asymmetry of hers in the nude, one breast hidden, the other exposed, giving her the look of a victorious reclining amazon: all that is mine, as the echo belongs to the voice. There is something else that is also mine, but it can't be seen, because her eyes are shut. Even if she were to open them, you couldn't see it, because it is in them deep down, fallen inward, forgotten, the way water forgets everything we've thrown into it, everything that disturbs it, tossing waves into ever widening circles and then settling to the bottom, flattened into a smooth, unruffled surface. I can barely see Livia's face: superimposed are so many hurried kisses of mine, mine alone, so many brief encounters as I rested my eyes on the small, oval contours of the very features I see, kept alive on faith alone in the Livia of flesh and blood, and now reflecting the face of another desperate creature, the face of my love for Livia. I see myself alive and awake, in the pathetic vigil of my farewell, in her sleeping face. I am in her for the last time. Because as soon as Livia opens her eyes, my destruction, slow and exhaustive, will begin, the ruin of my ephemeral work. The first thing Livia will take off will be the nudity that I spread over her body. And then, in front of the mirror, aided by an arsenal of lotions, creams and pencils, with great care she will furiously scrub me off her face, ruthlessly plucking out, kiss by kiss, all the passion I had lavished upon her. With red lipstick she will paint over my lips, pressed to her mouth and doubly indelible with that last kiss, a third draft of her lips, artificially penciled in. And finally, she will brandish, all metallic and gleaming like an invincible weapon, a silver comb in order to extricate herself from those poor, entangled embraces of mine, those deeply felt, secret spaces of the heart that had taken refuge in the winding strands of her hair, my own private maze. And there she stands before the mirror, I undone, she redone, transformed from what was an instant ago a richly passionate life held in my arms into an authorized biography, all imperfection deleted.

This imperfection is myself, written on her face, her flesh, and already erased, like an unwanted premature wrinkle. She will take away nothing of mine: she doesn't want it; she never wanted it. Which is to say she will take away the same things of mine she already had: my three books, nearly all memorized, what anyone could have, what anyone could buy without knowing me. She doesn't even want me to autograph them for her, as if she were afraid the ink from my pen, my very name, would leak beyond the book and seep into the page behind it: her heart, which no longer belongs to me and which is now completely blank. But as for the rest of those three hours, of every single day in the space of a month and a half (three identical and never-to-be-repeated hours, a few days spent here, flawless, inside, with a balcony that we first thought faced the afternoon, but as we were leaving, we see that it faced the night; three hours, another time, in an unending panorama that was rolled up like a reel of film in the landscape, and that she and I, alone in the car, would happily unwind, leaving them behind later, with their forests and castles, their sadness and Middle Ages, forgotten, skimmed quickly, like the descriptions of Sir Walter Scott; three hours, one afternoon, like pointed arches, without the direct light of day, illuminated like a missal by the thirteenth-century artist who authored the stained-glass windows, the two of us sitting on a cathedral bench; three hours, but only once, with striped awning, and a name written on both sides—"Mon plaisir"—which I move forward, accelerating from time to time with the oars, on the Rhine, or let float, when Livia orders me to, over the ripples like a weightless, airy happiness, which will never sink and in which the two of us have embarked), as for each of these three hours, she will take away nothing.

Deep down maybe she's doing it out of fairness, out of a sense of justice, and she doesn't want anything of mine because she hasn't left me anything of hers either. Put another way, she doesn't want to leave me anything. She gave me what you see there, asleep and rose-colored, in the bed. And when she gave it to me, I believed it was a token, a solemn and symbolic surrender, an advance payment and pledge of the total contribution. But that's as far as she let me go. I'm saying it badly: so that I would not go beyond her limits, she placed herself outside them, on the border of her being, leaving only her body. And so, like a country that displays all its charms in cities near the border, I no longer have a reason to go any further. It would be ridiculous to say that she has closed off the path to her heart. No, she wore it, generously, all at once, on her flesh; it was more naked than the body itself, visible and without mystery. So much so that I no longer see her, and when I kiss her, the only contact I feel is her delightful, physical reality. Then my dissatisfaction, a tenaciously held, tyrannical dissatisfaction that goes way back, back to the long-standing definition, "Man is compounded of body and soul," began to function, and I fabricated a soul for her in my own way, as you might reassemble with a few vague gestures of marble, scattered throughout museums

57

and headless, a scene from the creation. So I made her soul from within, and I have it here, hypothetical and reconstructed, as I stand trembling all over at this restoration of a work of art, so close yet lost to me.

Yes, that's the way it has to be. She is hiding her soul from me out of modesty, out of reserve, or maybe pride; I don't know why. But I have persisted and found it at last and I have it here; it's hers and mine. So you see, she will leave me—she who doesn't want to leave me anything—her soul, which is at the same time my work, in my hands. How wonderful it would have been, if she had only let me try it on her one day! This soul, made to measure, with scrupulous care, with nothing omitted, neither the narrow, slender line of the hips, nor the changing color of her eyes, nor the slightly immoderate length of her calves, I am certain that it could have been adjusted, intangible and very tightly fitted like desire, to her bodily form. Happy day, Livia's day, perfect and complete! But now what am I going to do? I shall be left with this uncommissioned soul I have made, and she will have fled with a hypothetical and provisional one and it will be impossible to make any comparisons with the genuine article. And so this trembling reality will end up being, for lack of a body, a creation of my fantasy, a work of literature. If I could only try it out, now that she is asleep, as a surprise! Even though she'd never find out, just so that I could rid myself of this piercing doubt of "what would it be like . . ." But it isn't going to be possible. I would have to move her a little, check to see if it slips in nicely into the very marrow of the arm, that's the arm I made, long and rosy, which just happens to be thrown across the pillow. More than anything, I'd have to raise her eyelids and see if the two eyes of the soul, mine and Livia's, fit in their orbit, the most delicate and exquisite part of my work, the centerpiece of my reconstruction. It isn't possible: interposed between her original soul, asleep within a dream, and this very exact and tender replica I've brought there is a body, impassible, exhausted, inert, which is the supreme resistance, because it has just surrendered to me.

Suddenly she stirs, like the sky at the first breeze of day, imperceptibly, no doubt because a small current of the awakening air is caressing her. She speaks, murmurs something. I come to her anxiously. I have a presentiment that her soul, now that it is absent and abandoned, is about to appear, like a captive in a ballad when the Moorish guard goes away, here on her lips, making the encounter possible. I come closer, holding in my hand this soul of my making, to see if this way they will meet as equals, within one all-encompassing soul, hers and mine, finally. But no. Her body returns, scarcely having quivered, to its original repose. And the two words that smiling escaped from her lips, instead of clarifying everything, have left me in the dark. Because they are two very strange words: my name, Melchor, and united to it for the first time in my life, another unknown name: Susana. She said: "Melchor, Susana." I retreat, beaten, vacilating. This new piece of information—Susana—which evidently is anchored deep in her heart, messes up everything. I will have to remake her soul, taking this new factor into account. But what, who is she, this Susana? There is no time even for me to ask because Livia is waking up. The light, like a little girl taking advantage of any distraction in order to go play in the street, has gone outside when I wasn't looking. Night has fallen. And for a moment, until Livia turns on the electricity, there is no other light in the room or in my heart, except the white radiance of her naked body.

The desire was here, hidden and crouched low in the most secret corner of my heart, shaking, wanting to go to the station with Livia, to see her leave: a shrinking desire that doesn't dare show itself, not even in the eyes, knowing very well the horror she has of sentimental scenes and melodrama. But this is the strange, the surprising part of her leaving: Livia slips easily into my heart, arriving silken and sure of herself, just like a ferret to the den of my desire, and taking hold of that timid and frightened little beast, she brings it to me in her mouth, her lips, her words, offering it to the same breast that suckled it, as if it were her own desire.

"I want you to come to the station."

And night itself begins to glow, shedding its evening black for the deep shaded wrap of her going away. It isn't a diffuse and amorphous light, vaguely outlined and romantic like moonlight, but cutout, concrete, transformed into sequined words endowed with the stringent and surprising poetry of that luminous announcement: "I want you to come to the station." I timidly suggest picking her up at her house, but smiling, she firmly puts me aright:

"No, it's better if we go separately. The train leaves at 1:35, so that means you can come at . . ."

Livia stops short, hesitating. She wavers. And not only does the thread of her voice break off on her lips, and the beat of my heart, but I see that everything around me obeys in a cosmic pause, and comes to a halt, hanging on what Livia has to say. Cars hit their brakes squealing; then an enormous omnibus crashes against the curb; the Negro in the jazz band at the Café Inglés stands on the terrace with his mouth open, cry hanging in the

59

air; and the municipal clock winds down, stopped for exactly the length that she pauses, fifteen seconds.

"All right. . . , you can come . . . one minute before."

Traffic resumes, motors vibrate, the world turns, and the cry of the singer pierces sharply like a black-headed needle the soft blue pincushion of the September sky. And Livia disappears, light as a leaf, swept away by the wave of a "Good-bye," sharp and not quite final, which spatters my face with tiny, caressing good-byes like drops of water.

I stand here on the sidewalk of the boulevard, balancing myself on this rope stretched over a void called "one minute before." Two or three pedestrians run into me, practically knock me down, believing no doubt that I am an absent-minded man, as I block the way in the middle of the sidewalk. They don't realize that I am involved in a very delicate and heart-wrenching investigation: finding out how much time Livia really means by giving me one minute to say good-bye. Quite obviously, one minute is either nothing or everything. I will have to fix reference marks, a starting point for the finish line. I take out my watch: eight o'clock. Of course it's clear I ought not to go to the station before twelve. So I have four hours to go. Nevertheless, Livia hesitated quite a bit . . . and anyway, the station is a long way off. I will definitely go at twelve, even if it is a little early. But for that I will have to leave the city at half past eleven. (I discover to my surprise that the four hours are already minus thirty minutes.) I don't know if I'll find a taxi; I will have to go look for one at the club. And as the club is far from where I live—twenty minutes away—I'll leave the house at eleven. (The four hours have now been reduced to three.) I'll go the long way around, by the river, even though it's a little slower: I'll have to move up my departure to half past ten. But, in that case, I only have a little more than two hours in order to dress and eat . . . and I surprise myself suddenly with a whistle on my lips and the cane raised high to stop a passing taxi. The strange thing is that I don't give the driver my home address, but inexplicably, precisely these instructions: "I'm in a hurry, to the East Station restaurant." And then I collapse against the back seat, voluptuously breathing in not the perfume of the municipal garden we are whizzing past, but the delicious aroma of this nearly intoxicating, firmly reasoned decision of mine: "In the long run, the best thing to do is that: just go and eat at the station restaurant. That way I'm already there, and I don't have to wait more than a minute." Because I have decided that the minute before the Prague Express arrives is to begin now, at 8:05.

"I just got here," I answer Livia with studied indifference, who asks me if I've been waiting very long when she turns up in the enormous waiting room of the station, at 1:25. She's already wearing her traveling face, an impersonal and anonymous face purposely made for circulating a few hours among strangers in a train. She thus becomes a simple passenger who reserves her vast repertoire of authentic gestures for the moment of departure and arrival. Even from afar this confers the cool, haughty air of a queen upon her, decoratively corroborated because she appears at the head of a retinue of slaves, all bent under the weight of a huge number of packages, luggage, suitcases, hat boxes, and parading as in a frieze, under her pharaonic surveillance in order to set up a pyramid of travel objects on the floor of the station platform. Now Livia leans over to look for something in a little handbag. I don't know if it is because her cheeks redden with the effort, or because she was carrying her real face hidden inside and had just put it on again for her departure, the fact is that she looks at me the way she has always looked at me, the way she will never look at me again (she is going to leave at any moment). And she says to me:

"Why don't we sit in the waiting room, I have to talk to you."

The room, in an exotic caprice of the company, not entirely unjustified since the line ends in Constantinople, is decorated in oriental style. There's no doubt the setting is a definite influence: it makes Livia think that this is one of those thousand-and-one nights, granting her the provisional and momentary role of Scheherazade, and inspiring in her, not a confession or those last, conclusive words, maybe the supreme revelation I was expecting, but an unexpected, surprising story to which I listen, completely astonished. It is the story of a marvelous girl. She possesses all the attributes of perfection: cultivated, both acquired and unacquired, with a splendid natural beauty and superimposed on it, another beauty, fabricated yet all her own; everything that can be seen and experienced is there, standing behind her, and another, impending world she is going to invent is right in sight of her twenty-five years. As a coquettish touch to her perfection one small defect, myopia, without which she would be inaccessible, superhuman, pure perfection. The enthusiasm with which Livia speaks of her (she tells me she is her best friend) is so effective, so infectious, that I see her emerge little by little out of nothingness, assume a form, take on life. And when Livia puts her hand in her bag, I don't doubt that it is to pull out already complete, the only thing missing, the person herself, or at the very least, her photographic effigy. But that isn't it. What Livia shows me is a little slip of blue paper, a telegram where I read: "Arrive tonight, 1:35. Susana." Because her friend's name, Livia explains, is Su-

61

sana. I, although immobile, quiet, on the thousand-and-one-nights divan, am in reality making desperate efforts, with my hands, with my reason, with my memory, to get out of this mess in which Livia has entangled me, her final betrayal, wherein she intends to leave me choking, a prisoner in the enigma woven with these threads of two colors: Livia, Susana (Susana, the name of this afternoon, Livia, her best friend. . . , inexplicable then that she should go when the other is coming . . . maybe . . .). But no: the imbroglio expands prodigiously; I am lost in it, give up trying to solve it, and clamor, deep inside, for an incisive blade of steel to cut (to loosen it is impossible) this Gordian knot. And as it is 1:35, the machine that is the Prague Express comes to cut it, sharp, metallic and sweeping, entering and dominating through force, like an athlete in an exhibition.

We move toward each other. At a small window the slender, curved form of a woman leans out and sees Livia. As though she were afraid the train would keep on going and she might not have the chance to give it to her, she hastily tosses her an immense and sudden smile, which because of the speed is very badly directed and strikes me instead right in my breast. It is so dense, so filled, that it makes me reel, almost knocks me over, with a brand-new pain in the heart. When I recover, I see that Livia and Susana, hand in hand, smiling and sisterly, are advancing toward me, as from the depths of an unknown mythology, nymphs liberated from the iron dragon-train that had held one of them captive. They are bounding forward in the initiation of an adventure without borders, the introduction of the new friend. But unfortunately, the myth never gives up a victim, and the price for the rescue of that soul coming from Paris is the body that is embarking with the ritual introductions scarcely made, no time for any more, in one leap onto the Prague train. And in that leap of Livia's, apparently free and joyful, onto the coach car, in that voluntary and happy surrender to the monster, I see, in a final and blinding revelation, the fated offering, the sacrifice offered on the altar of something superior and perfect, of something that is going to begin now. Just as the train starts up, with a pace as rhythmic and solid as a sentence of Sophocles, and I remain alone with Susana on the platform, I realize that the soul I made for Livia, that profound and perfect soul, in my image and likeness, soul of my passion, did not belong to her. It is precisely, without a wrinkle, without a flaw, the one predestined, the only one meant for this marvelous body that has just liberated itself from the cyclops with the enormous shining eye: the Prague Express, the express that is carrying away on its black hump, on its deafening whistle, my Livia Schubert, once and for always incomplete.

Víspera del gozo

Mundo cerrado

Pasó dos horas leyendo. Junto a él, en el asiento, estaba cerrado el libro. Un libro de letra clara, amplio margen, asunto intrincado y atractivo, de esos que compramos un día de invierno pensando en leerle aquella noche al amor del fuego, pero que luego, a las primeras líneas, se comprende que ha sido escrito para otro lugar y sazón: para una tarde clara de viaje, y que sólo entonces nos dará un placer totalmente exprimido y sabroso. Aunque luego suele ocurrir que en el viaje a que estaba destinado demos con un compañero de buen habla y se pase todo el tiempo en charlar, mientras el libro sigue abandonado, desoído el grito amarillo y pertinaz de su cubierta, como una virgen desdeñada, sobre los almohadones. Y así pasó esta vez; porque las dos horas de lectura lo fueron sin libro delante, con la vista puesta en un cristal—el de la ventanilla—, y lo leído, imposible de encajar en ningún género literario: Andrés leía un paisaje nuevo, una nación desconocida. Cierto que la lectura no se hacía a su grado y voluntad, porque él no podía pasar las hojas, y esta misión era ejercida, con velocidades toscamente desiguales, por el maquinista, el cual, sin duda por ser nuevo en la línea, ignoraba la profunda belleza de lo que iba revelando con torpísimo ritmo. Llegaba, por ejemplo, una página tierna, conmovedora, tan clásica en su sencillez cual la despedida homérica, escrita con cristalina frase por el curso del río, toda sembrada—como de acertados epítetos—de arbolado y verdura, con dos o tres imágenes soberbias, puras e irisadas nubes, coronando el período, y el tren la volvía rápidamente, a noventa kilómetros, sin tiempo apenas para leerla completa, cuando menos para aprenderla de memoria y llevársela adentrada, como deseó al ojearla, el corazón. Y en cambio, cinco minutos más tarde, el tren se estaba parado un rato en una página de estación de tercera, donde una vía muerta, con despintados vagones, una pared gris, de depósitos, al fondo, y un cartel: «Lampistería», por lema componían un «trozo» asombrosamente realista, eso sí, pero tan pobre e insignificante, que no se le explicaba uno como nacido del mismo autor, sospechando en él una interpolación apócrifa. Si aquel arroyuelo que descendía casi en cascada le prometía de

65

lejos y por los ojos una cadena de ritmos peregrinos y libres, luego, al pasar junto a él, el maquinista, so pretexto de que cruzaban el puente, desencadenaba un fragor metálico donde se ahogaba de sequedad la gracia del agua. Otra vez cortó un delicadísimo trino de pájaro, salvado por milagro del ruido de la marcha, exquisitamente iniciado como una adolescencia, con un pitido brutal y agudo, el cual no podía tener más objeto que el de arrojar en las almas románticas de unas señoritas habitantes en aquella capital de cuarta clase, ya muy próxima, la visión bisemanal e idealizada del tren de lujo, del rápido de las cuatro, que llevaba colgando, a la cabeza y a la cola, dos grandes ciudades. Y tan inoportuno y fatal como esas preocupaciones súbitas que nos asaltan en medio de una lectura, sin saber de dónde vienen, porque un viento de dentro las empuja, e interponen entre nuestra atención y lo escrito un elemento extraño e impenetrable, la locomotora, inesperadamente, lanzaba aquí, hacia nuestro lado y ayudada por el viento, ahora de fuera, un humo gris y apelmazado, detrás del cual estaba huyendo vertiginosamente, expirando sin remedio, para nosotros, quizá la escena más hermosa del libro. Y aun lo peor de todo fue aquella vez, cuando se desplegaba en su cimera belleza una descripción de desfiladero abrupto, todo rocas y nácar, y de pronto se cerró bruscamente el relato y quedó el cristal de la ventanilla ilegible, negro, con hosca negrura de túnel, en un túnel. Ya aquello le cansó, le molestó en su dignidad de aficionado rico y ocioso que lee y goza a su capricho. Y sin hacer caso del silbido con que el tren le invitaba, a la salida del túnel, a reanudar la arbitraria lectura, echó mano al maletín y sacó sus dos abultados cuadernos de señas.

Porque desde algún tiempo atrás tenía costumbre de registrar los nombres y residencias de sus amigos, por partida doble, en dos libretas. En la primera estaban anotados por orden alfabético de apellidos, como suele hacer todo el mundo. Pero en la segunda el encabezamiento de cada página correspondía a una ciudad, que llevaba a renglón seguido la lista de los conocidos que allí tenía. Andrés, extraordinariamente aficionado a ciudades y caracteres, tímido y curioso, a la par amigo de la compañía y de la íntima soledad, hallaba en este sistema de los dos cuadernos interdependientes un mecanismo perfecto, dos ruedas dentadas, gracias a cuyo engranaje, casi siempre fortuito e irregular, se decidía un día a tomar la mala de Indias o el Oriente Expreso. Lo nuevo, lo desconocido, lo temerosamente deseado y distante, tales ciudades, apuntadas en el segundo cuaderno, sólo cobraba movimiento y vida gracias a la rotación que le imprimiera lo sabido, lo familiar, los nombres del cuaderno primero. Conocer personas, saber que un amigo había mudado de residencia era para él una ampliación del mundo posible. Y su vida, semejante a un progreso hacia una cartografía geográfico-sentimental, completa y sin huecos, donde no hubiese tierras incógnitas, donde cada ciudad, por enorme y remota que fuese tuviera su explicación y franquía en un nombre, en un ser humano, en el recuerdo de un amor o una amistad. Tal lugar, famoso en la historia y en el arte, no lo había visitado: no conocía a nadie allí. Pero un día, un compañero de colegio le comunicaba su traslado a aquella legación. Y partía a la conquista de la ciudad inmensa, sin más armas que unas señas apuntadas en un librito, pero tan confiado como el multimillonario que acaricia la llave minúscula y acerada gracias a la cual se abrirá sin obstáculo y sin pena la enorme puerta de su departamento de caudales. Otra vez, en un hotel, conocía a una muchacha nacida y avecindada en una ciudad menor de un país histórico, ciudad que se la había aparecido hasta hoy como una isla codiciadera e inaccesible, apresada en un cuadro de primitivo, ya fuera del tiempo, sin navío que le llevara. Y, de pronto, aquel punto lejano se acercaba al alcance de su voluntad, por modo mágico y suavísimo, igual que se presenta el cisne de *Lohengrin,* todo porque una señorita muy blanca, de ademanes ondulosos y menudos, como de pluma, le dijo una tarde: «Venga usted a pasar unos días. Yo le enseñaré mi pueblo». Desde aquel instante, las cincuenta mil almas que el censo atribuía a aquel lugar, hasta entonces dormidas en un largo encantamiento, despertaban, devueltas a sus faenas cotidianas y multicolores, con calidad de gente que nos mirará pasar muy pronto al lado de nuestra amiga. Y al escribir en el segundo cuaderno los dos nombres—ciudad, amigo—juntos y maridados, como en esas tarjetas de los nuevos matrimonios, un punto concreto del mundo se desnudaba de aprensión, de velada reserva y amenaza, y, coincidiendo con aquella oferta, se inauguraba alegremente una línea de ferrocarril, hecha hace cincuenta años, usada ya por tantos trenes.

Miró el nombre de la ciudad adonde se dirigía ahora: *Icosia.* Capital menor de Europa, de un encanto elegante, tímido y reposado, como el de esa hermana pequeña de una beldad famosa, menos guapa, menos inteligente, pero que, sin embargo, tiene siempre un semblante sonriente y feliz, una expresión secundaria y muy suya. Junto a Icosia había algo escrito y borrado, cual una esperanza que se abandona, y luego, con letra muy reciente: Lady Gurney. Sonrió. Porque, en realidad, a esta amiga, Lady Gurney, que le allanaba el acceso a Icosia, no la conocía. Coqueteaba con esta realidad, la acariciaba sin miedo, como un revólver descargado y de lujo, que no puede hacer daño: «No conozco a Lady Gurney. Tengo muchos retratos suyos, por esa manía de retratarse continuamente. Aquél tan bonito con el traje de noche que llevó al baile de Trinity, el único que no se hizo por su gusto, sino porque se lo pedí yo. Pero el mejor de todos es ese en que estamos los dos juntos, el día de las regatas Oxford-Cambridge, aquel día del beso suyo, sin respuesta. Tiene escrito detrás un verso de Swinburne, no recuerdo cuál ... Es divertido pensar que no conozco a Lády Gurney». Y lanzaba al aire la contradicción, la hacía volar al modo de un humo de cigarrillo impulsado por su aliento en la atmósfera tibia y recatada del vagón, siguiéndola voluptuosamente, invisible, con la vista. ¿Cómo sería Lady Gurney? Ojos pardos, ¿de qué color ahora? Andar suyo, breve, enérgico, y quizá hoy conquistado, cual por un ritmo misterioso y lejano, sólo por ella percibido, a insólitas languideces y *ritardandos.* ¿Y la sonrisa de ayer, seca, intermitente, sin misterio, quizá, agrandada, expresiva y honda, clavada siempre en el rostro, disponible a cualquier momento, sin necesidad de acecho y salto, como antes? Aquella evocación de Lady Gurney le causó un súbito malestar. Y como se arranca del rostro amado y sabido el antifaz de seda tras el cual nos hablaba un momento, coqueteando, y nos parecía otra y desconocida, tiró por la ventanilla el nombre nuevo y conyugal, Lady Gurney, que sólo tenía seis semanas de vida, y se encontró detrás, palpitante y estremecida, con Alice Chesterfield, soltera Lady Gurney, que le tendía los dos brazos constantes de la amistad antigua. Aunque era inútil querer engañarse, y el cuaderno decía la estricta verdad, Alice Chesterfield escrito antes y al lado, borrado aquello, Lady Gurney. Habría que pasarse la realidad como una punta de acero, aguda y dolorosa, una pluma, por el corazón para tachar algo, a ejemplo del cuaderno. Tacharía dos años de vida, en Londres, en Cambridge, en Ramsgate, dos años de ...

«¿El señor se queda en Icosia Playa o en Icosia Ciudad?»

La pregunta del empleado, brusca y disyuntiva, como unas tijeras, cortó el monólogo interior, le dejó trunco, en dos pedazos el mejor y más sabroso, el que quedaba dentro, el del recuerdo inexpresado.

«En Icosia Ciudad.»

Aquí vivía el reciente marido de Alicia, Lord Gurney, aquí vivía, no más que dos semanas su amiga casada. Y como uno de esos regalos que se cruzan, por motivo matrimonial, Alicia y su esposo le habían ofrecido Icosia, ciudad menuda y frutal, antes altísima, pendida en una rama inaccesible, rama que ahora Lord y Lady Gurney sujetaban acercándola a tierra, de modo que su amigo pudiese coger sin esfuerzo el fruto madurado a fuerza de tantas primaveras con nostalgia. Ya le pareció a Andrés que sentía en la boca un sabor deliciosamente nuevo, el zumo de Icosia. En efecto, por la ventanilla empezaron a entrar alocadas, aleteando, como esas gaviotas terreras que nos indican que el mar está ya aquí, aunque no le veamos, palabras heráldicas y anunciadoras escritas en grandes carteles: «Icosia, 10 kilómetros», «Omnium-Bazar. Esta semana: ropa blanca», «Pears, Pears, Pears», «Icosia, 5 kilómetros», y luego, sin letrero, anónima y evidente, pero a pedazos porque entera no cabía, la ciudad misma. Pasaron por entre dos largas filas de vagones, esos pobres vagones de tercera o de mercancías que se agolpan por las tardes a los dos lados de la ruta señalada por los programas oficiales, como el pueblo ocioso de una gran ciudad esperando la llegada del rey extranjero, para ver entrar soberbio, raudo y brillante, el rápido de Viena. Ya salía a su encuentro la estación central, con un ademán acogedor, gris y eléctrico, hecho de arcos voltaicos, de reflejos en los rieles, de oficiosas ofertas de los mozos. Unas pocas personas esperaban; entre ellas buscó Andrés la figura de Alicia. Y eso porque es tal la fuerza de la costumbre que se le había olvidado que estaba casada y los ojos rutinarios y torpes buscaban una silueta sola en vez de la pareja que debía esperarle. Pero no encontró nada, a nadie. Descendió del coche. Y de pronto vio allí, en el andén, una carta para él. ¿Cómo la había conocido? Porque el sobre no mostraba la letra redonda y muelle, tan familiar de Alicia, sino una escritura angulosa y extraña. Sin embargo, estaba seguro de que aquel lacayo alto y serio que la llevaba en la mano, completando así su gesto indagador le buscaba a él. Así era.

«Esta carta de parte de Lord Gurney. El coche espera afuera al señor». No quiso leerla allí mismo. «Vamos». Al salir de la estación no vio nada, ni siquiera la avenida corta y voluptuosa, toda florida de acacias, como esa mirada con que una mujer o una ciudad nos invita a seguirla, a ir más allá. Toda su alma se le había ido escurriendo hacia la mano y estaba allí pesando y sopesando la carta cerrada, tiesa, gravosa, indudablemente con algo inmenso dentro. Ya en el coche la abrió: «. . . Alicia ha muerto anteayer. Le espero aquí, en el campo . . .» Icosia, al primer contacto con los labios, apenas mordida le daba el sabor más amargo de todos, sabor a tierra mortal. Se la arrancó de la boca, la tiró por la ventanilla al valle verde, donde se quedó toda brillante, como una fruta pútrida y engañosa. Porque el automóvil, sin penetrar en la ciudad, habiéndola también mordisqueado apenas, corría ya hacia el campo, volviendo la espalda a los adioses inclinados de los cipreses del cementerio, en la colina.

Entrada en Sevilla

Salieron a las seis de la tarde, cuando el sol de aquella calle estaba ya un poco cansado. Se le habían rendido los aceros matinales en vanas porfías por entrarse en los recatados interiores domésticos. Como era un sol de mayo, acalorado de su propio fuego, soñaba con tenderse a la sombra, en un patio, en una cámara, en cualquiera de aquellos lugares umbrosos que tan excelentemente le defendían contra su mismo ardor, y donde se debía de estar tan a gusto, sin sol. Probó todo, velas y cierros, zaguanes y ventanos. Todo impenetrable. Los toldos dorados en los patios, los macizos portones entornados, y en los balcones y miradores, visillos rígidos y blancos, que se le negaban como vírgenes fuertes. Si una vez se deslizó furtivamente por un alto ventanillo descuidado, tuvo mala ventura porque fue a caer en la superficie hostil y lisa de un espejo, de donde, herido por sus mismos filos, multiplicado en visos y reflejos, salió rebotando, maltrecho, arrastrándose por las paredes, fugitivo de su propia imagen. Y tuvo que estarse todo el día en una calle soleada, melancólicamente derribada por tierra su rubia melena leonina, y tan olvidado y desdeñoso ahora ya, que las sombras avanzaban con paso quedo de traidor melodramático, afilando el frío puñal del crepúsculo, sin que él las sintiera.

Claudio bajó la escalera, y atravesó el patio que tenía un frescor y un son de agua, y todo su encanto sostenido milagrosamente, como una arquitectura excesiva, en la varilla vacilante y cristalina de un surtidor. Había para salir un portal oscuro y bajo, pero como la luz exterior era más esperanzada y definida que la del patio, Claudio no pasó por esa sensación diminutiva y un poco triste de cuando se sale, y antes al contrario, le pareció que entraba en alguna parte: en efecto, iba a entrar en la ciudad codiciada, en Sevilla. Pero, por lo pronto, lo que al fondo del zaguán se apercibía, no era paisaje de ciudad, sino la poderosa forma de un automóvil en espera, que lo tapaba todo. Más de cerca vio Claudio que al otro lado del coche, sin dejar casi espacio para el paso de una persona, se alzaba ya la fachada de la casa frontera; y el automóvil tenía que estar tan pegado a la puerta, que el primer paso que dio Claudio en Sevilla no tuvo para sustento blanda tierra andaluza, sino una faja neutra de nacionalidad lejana, un estribo de automóvil. «Aquí los señores no pisan suelo», dijo Robledo, advertida y sonriente. Y mientras ella se cubría con la fina manta, Claudio, torciendo mucho la cabeza, miró la fachada de la desconocida casa de donde salían. Cuando llegaron a ella, unas horas antes, era de noche, así que con haber sido tan feliz en su seno aún no la había visto. Y la miró como se mira a una persona a la que conocemos muy bien interiormente, porque nos escribió muchas cartas, o porque nos hablaron largamente de ella, al verla por primera vez, buscando ávidamente en su rostro corroboración o desencanto. Pero nada le dijo, porque era una casa atractiva y reservada. La fachada blanca, ahora en sombra, mate y sin relumbre. Los dos balcones, el cierro, tenían una alegría sencilla y popular, de copla, pintada de verde en los barrotes, pero los visillos almidonados y tiesos la corregían apagadamente como una interpretación académica. En la baranda de la azotea había flores, sí, inmensas flores azules y blancas, pero sin estremecimiento ni olor, porque estaban puestas a salvo de toda contingencia y peligro, de sazón y desazón, sin primavera ni agosto, pintadas, secas y brillantes, en uno barrocos remates de cerámica. Todo en la apariencia de la casa era como las alegrías y el amor de dentro, anoche, delicioso y mal explicado. De pronto el automóvil al primer arranque se dejó aquello atrás. La casa se volvió una blancura estriada de verde, y desapareció prestamente, sin esfuerzo, rezagada en la visión y en la memoria como una isla o un recuerdo que se hunde sin rastro de la tierra o el placer que fueron. «Fíjate bien, ésta es Sevilla», dijo Robledo.

El auto ceñido estrechamente a derecha e izquierda por casas, empezaba su heroico viaje. La calle, inmóvil, pero poseída con la marcha del coche de una actividad vertiginosa y teatral, empezó a desplegar formas, líneas, espacios multicolores y cambiantes, rotos, reanudados a cada instante, sin coherencia alguna, y con idéntica rapidez y destreza con que muestra un prestimano los colorinescos objetos que le van a servir en su juego, más que para que el público los vea, con el malicioso propósito de que su rauda sucesión cree una imagen confusa y apta para cualquier engaño en la mirada del espectador. Sí, probablemente en cuanto todo aquello se aquietara, de esta confusión de colores iba a salir limpia y total, Sevilla, ofrecida como en la palma de una mano hábil en la llanada del Guadalquivir. Pero por ahora no se veía ni ciudad, ni calles, ni siquiera sus últimos elementos, casas. Todo lo que aprehendían los ojos eran fragmentos, cortes y paños de muros, rosa, verde, azul, y de trecho en trecho, como un punto redondo y negro que intenta dar apariencias de orden a una prosa en tumulto, un portal en el que se hundía la mirada siempre demasi-

71

ado tarde, porque apenas llegada a la cancela y dudosa de por cuál de aquellos geométricos pasajes entraría en el presentido patio, ya empezaba de nuevo otra cosa, dejándose atrás aquélla: una pared de colores, la arista de una esquina brusca, una reja, cerrada casi siempre, pero que una vez mostró con patética prisa, cautiva detrás de sus barrotes como una gacela, una luz tiernísima y sin nadie, de cuarto habitado, de cuarto de donde se acaba de ir, adonde volverá dentro de un momento alguien que nunca veremos. De pronto, en un cruce, la calle por donde iban hizo un esguince, se torció a la derecha, escapó, toda ondulada y colorinesca, como una huída de gitana. Pero no: se había equivocado la vista. Esa calle fugitiva era otra y no la suya, otra que arrancaba de allí y se confundía con ella, toda igual y deliciosamente distinta, y por eso el corazón creyó que la perdía, dudoso y engañado como aquella mañana en que siguió a la hermana de la mujer querida unos instantes, por la semejanza a lo lejos, de sus siluetas.

De cuando en cuando miraba hacia arriba: precipitado desfile de miradores torcidos, de balcones desenfocados, todos herméticos y sin gente; y más alto el cielo, vereda azul, escasa y blanda, entre márgenes de claveles y geranios, por las macetas de las azoteas, veredita estrecha por lo que habría de caminarse de uno en uno, y aun así imposible de pasar ahora, porque en medio se había dormido, aplomada y quieta, una aborregada nube sin oficio. Se le desvanecía a Claudio la Sevilla convencional de los panoramas, definición lejana en el paisaje con dos líneas—caserío, Giralda— que se cortan con una belleza estrictamente geométrica. La ciudad no se definía, lejos, depurada y distinta, sino que vivía, cerca, complicadísima, esquiva siempre a la línea recta, complacida como cuerpo de bailarina en gentiles quiebros y sinuosidades. Sus intenciones mudaban rumbo constantemente, y a fuerza de no querer nada seguido, de cambiar sin tregua, mostraban una voluntad poderosa y en el fondo rectilínea, de suerte que sobreponiéndose al albedrío humano, no iba el hombre en ningún momento allí donde su propósito le impulsara, sino donde el capricho de la ciudad, su alma voluntariosa e indómita, le atrajera, para placer o dolor—exquisita duda—con halagueros y variados recursos itinerarios. Imposible estarse quieto aquí en estas calles onduladas y penetrantes como frases nocturnas. Pero imposible, luego, ir a parte alguna, servirse de aquellos viales para el logro de un designio insertándolos en calidad de medios en una empresa racional superior a su complicada norma. Había que andar por Sevilla, abandonado, como flotante en aguas invisibles de estos cauces secos, marchar sin adonde, querer ir, pero sin ninguna llegada, arrastrado por estas corrientes sin caudal, en un automóvil, góndola sin rumbo, a la deriva. ¿Dónde estaría Sevilla? Sin duda por estas venas azules, por estas venas rosadas, que no tenían nombre de venas, sino de calles andaluzas—Aromo, Lirio, Escarpín—, se había de llegar a su corazón recóndito y difícil. Cada visión nueva era la aventura final, el último encantamiento, y, sin embargo, a cada visión se sustituía inmediatamente la de al lado, lo mismo que huye una nota de la cuerda donde nació, porque en la voluntad del ejecutante ya hay otra esperando, que la alcanza y la completa. Y era preciso que la imaginación juntase tal trozo de blanqueada pared, aquel zaguán, una cancela, con la perspectiva no suya—ésta ya se había evadido—, sino de la casa vecina, y poniendo sobre todo eso balcones y terrazas ajenos y un ciel visible pero convencional, reconstruyese idealmente lo que por angostura de la calle y rapidez de la marcha no cabía, verdadero, en la visión. Y por eso la ciudad, tan real, tenía un temblor de fantasmagoría, un inminente peligro de que al no poder tenerse juntos, arbitrariamente ensamblados en la imaginación todos aquellos fragmentos que en realidad estaban perfectamente unidos, se viniera todo abajo, en un terremoto ideal y pintarrajeado como los que se muestran con comento de romances en los cartelones de las ferias. Estaba viendo Sevilla y aún tenía que seguir imaginándola, y la ciudad le era, tan dentro de ella, algo incierto e inaprehensible como una mujer amada, producto de datos reales, pero dispersos y nebulosos, y unificadora, lúcida fantasía que los coordina en superior encanto.

Sintió gana de mirar más de cerca, de bajar del auto. Pero en el mismo momento en que iba a decirlo así, a una vuelta brusca del coche el bolso de Robledo cayó al suelo y se desparramaron sus contenidos bienes. Robledo y Claudio se inclinaron al mismo tiempo para recoger las cosas caídas; fue largo, hubo que quitar la manta, explorar en los rincones y, como se tocaron sus manos, ver subir el color al rostro pálido de Robledo, verle luego irse avergonzado de sí mismo, blanca otra vez, por rubor del rubor. Al finalizar el episodio, Claudio, que no había perdido de vista en la memoria la calle dislocada y multicolor, se encontró, como la última cosa perdida en el fondo del auto, con su deseo de bajar, y dijo, antes de alzar la cabeza: «Oye, ¿por qué no ir un rato a pie, por aquí?» «¿Por aquí?—contestó Robledo—. Si esto es muy feo.» Incorporado ya, miró alrededor suyo: en efecto, era muy feo. En los dos minutos de la busca, casas de colores, calles, Sevilla, todo había desaparecido, entrevisto y maravilloso, vuelto acaso a la caja de engaños del prestimano, delicia huída. Y ahora estaban en una calle ancha, de trazado moderno, con altas casas grises, y al fondo el campo, fin de Sevilla. El asombro y el dolor de Claudio iban a quedarse sin expresión, cuando de pronto la bocina del auto, comunicada por misterioso conducto con su corazón, lanzó un rugido plañidero y ronco, disfrazado de aviso el inexperto transeúnte, pero en el que se reconocía, muy clara, hoy y empapada de siglos, la desesperación impotente y grandiosa con que el burlado egipán ve cómo se le escapa de nuevo la ninfa esquiva y deseada.

Cita de los tres

Cuando Angel entró en la iglesia no eran más que las seis menos cuarto, pero ya empezaban a dar las seis. Porque la ciudad tenía, y ese era su más secreto encanto, la razón de que la vida fuese aquí tan holgada y generosa, un modo descuidado y señoril de contar el tiempo. Estaba Jorge avezado a vivir en lugares donde esa riqueza inagotable y fugitiva, perfectamente acuñada en diversos tipos de moneda, horas, minutos y segundos, era escrupulosamente medida y administrada, pieza a pieza, por los relojes y por el tráfico, por las faenas humanas y por el alumbrado municipal, de suerte que nunca podía haber error en la cuenta y toda criatura recibía su porción exacta, los sesenta minutos, odiosamente iguales de la hora, a cada hora. Sin comprender que había gente, todos los seres venturosos, que necesitaban mucho más, porque al vivir con el ritmo pródigo y acelerado de la felicidad, libertos de las servidumbres del cómo y del cuánto, se gastaban la hora alegremente, en cualquier cosa, en caprichos, besos o pereza, despilfarrándola en unos minutos, para quedarse en seguida con las manos vacías, sin nada. Mientras que los desgraciados, que por su parva exigencia vital podían contentarse con muy poco, estaban allí enfrente, pasando y repasando entre sus dedos exangües, los dorados minutos sobrados, contándolos uno a uno, sin saber qué hacerse con tanto dinero, porque no tenían en qué gastar, como esos ricachos norteamericanos que pasean melancólicamente por los grandes hoteles, apoyados en las muletas de la extravagancia y la filantropía, una riqueza sin objeto. Pero aquí, en Sarracín, nada de eso: el tiempo estaba desnudo y se comportaba liberal y graciosamente, como en una fiesta báquica el cuerpo que soltó corsé y tirantes, ligas y corchetes, todo lo que le ceñía oprimido y estricto y se muestra ahora desenvuelto y rosado sin dejar ya dudas respecto a su entrega total. Las horas tenían exquisitas dilataciones imprevistas, llegaban antes de llegar igual que llega la persona que esperamos mucho antes de que esté aquí, sólo con su silueta adelantándose, resbalando toda hacia nosotros por la pulida superficie de este puente que echamos sobre la distancia, a medias, de una sonrisa suya y otra nuestra, separados y unidas.

Y lo mismo al marcharse, cuando ya las creíamos definitivamente ausentes, retornaban, con cualquier pretexto, un olvido fingido, disfraz de su deseo de pasar un rato más con nosotros. Por eso en aquella ciudad a eso de las seis menos cuarto ya comenzaban a dar las seis.

Era en el reloj de San Esteban, el cual por estar empinado en lo más alto del caserío dominaba grandes horizontes y veía a las nubes, a los trenes y a las horas, antes que nadie, muy a distancia, en cuanto asomaban por el borde azulado del tiempo. Y aunque estuviesen muy remotas, con lejos difíciles de bruma o de noche, las veía certeramente sin confundir nunca el vuelo alto, solitario y aguileño de la una, con la pareja flechera y sensual, inseparables cigüeñas de torre, de las dos de la tarde, ni mucho menos con aquella alegre bandada desceñida y revoltosa de las doce, que allá a eso del mediodía, aparecían, brincando y saltarinas, como chiquillas escapadas de la escuela, aprendizas de la tabla de dividir el tiempo en un alto colegio celeste. Las seis de San Esteban eran, pues, las primeras que aparecían en lo alto de su torre, arracimadas, frescas y rojizas, como cerezas tempranas, signo jubiloso de los placeres agraces. Eran para todos los que esperaban algo, para los que tenían prisa de vivir. Ellos oían este reloj mejor que ninguno, y decían: «Ya son las seis», a sabiendas de que no era verdad; y dejando todo lo que tenían empezado, aquello que se hubiera podido acabar en diez minutos más, salían saltando escaleras abajo, contentos y precipitados, cual si fuesen a llegar tarde, muy conscientes del engaño, pero engañados, abriéndole así un atajo al tiempo, atajo que les evitaría el largo y penoso rodeo de las seis de verdad, llevándolos presta y secretamente al mismo sitio: donde ella, la esperada, no estaría aún, porque sabía muy bien que el reloj ese adelantaba diez minutos.

Luego a partir de estas primeras companadas la misma hora iba sonando en distintos relojes, idéntica y deliciosamente transformada como si unos celestiales dedos antojadizos se entretuvieran en arrancar a la ciudad que tenía azoteas blancas, teclas blancas, alternadas, desde arriba, con breves calles en sombra, teclas negras, unas improvisadas variaciones sobre un tema conocido y popular, y eso tan hábilmente, que las personas de oído poco ducho no reconocían a veces el motivo primero, por la destreza con que le mudaba de ritmo y tono el ejecutante, y se preguntaban dudosos qué hora sería esa que estaba dando. Así que las horas no caían, a pesar de venir de los altos campanarios, bruscamente centelleantes, sobre los mortales, sino que se acercaban jugueteando, habiendo llegado ya y sin llegar, sonrientes con la sonrisa de la posesión prometida, y distantes aún, acaso inaccesibles, igual que en el más sabio y delicioso *flirting*. Y el que tuviera

76

miedo de una hora determinada del día, al tímido que la esperase de golpe en el corazón siempre que le quedaba tiempo, gracias a aquellas nubecillas precursoras e inofensivas que anunciaban el arribo de la mala nube negra, la hora de la verdad, para guarecerse en una gran distracción, en un estrépito buscado y artificial donde no se oyese ni reloj ni recuerdo.

Por fin llegaban las seis, las seis auténticas, justas, legítimas hijas del meridiano. Pero ellas, que se habían anunciado por el previo envío de tantas hermanas bastardas y parecidas, todas muy alborotadoras, llegaban ahora envueltas en la más augusta dignidad de personas reales, sin duda para distinguirse de ellas, en silencio. Porque las seis en punto no sonaban, no daban en ningún reloj; las marcaba con sus agujas el único que vivía puntualmente, sin equivocarse nunca, el de la Audiencia, reloj mudo y sin campana, dechado perfecto de una justicia, casi divina, que no yerra nunca y se cumple en secreto. De modo que la hora cierta estaba allí, en lo callado, en lo sonoramente vacío e inexistente, pura y sin engaño, al modo de esas verdades que acaso son lo más exacto de nuestro yo, pero que precisamente por eso no pueden modularse en sonidos y se pasan la vida, como las princesas medievales, allá en los altos alcázares del mirar, esperando, en los ojos, o zahareñas y encerradas en las moradas interiores del corazón. Nadie, pues, oía la hora verdadera sino entre dos aproximaciones, un poco antes o un poco después. Pero ya estaba aquí, y todo el que la había esperado, porque tenía cita con las seis, a las seis, la estrechaba fresca y palpitante entre los brazos, apresurando un poco los besos porque sabían que no podría estar mucho rato, más de una hora con ellos. Y sin embargo no era así. Porque había relojes que, sin duda, por estar enclavados en viejas torres del XI, tenían ese andar lento y profundo de lo románico y retrasaban invariablemente, cargados de nostalgia, sin querer separarse del pasado. Y por virtud de esos relojes resultaba que a las siete todavía no se habían acabado las seis. Y la hora duraba en algunas parroquias, cinco, en otras diez minutos más, prolongación exquisita e inesperada, igual a ese cuarto de hora de retraso que trae siempre el tren cuando se marcha nuestro amigo, hurto hecho al tiempo, bien robado y bien guardado, que nunca recobrará, como Zeus, el hijo escapado.

A esas seis retrasadas, el último recurso, que flotaban perezosas en el aire líquido y transparente como restos del naufragio del tiempo, se asió Angel, desesperado, ansioso para no hundirse del todo en la certidumbre hondísima, fría y sin luz, como el fondo del mar, de que ya no vendría Matilde.

«Apenas si son las seis, decía, aún puede venir». Aunque él sabía que las seis estaban allí hacía diez minutos, como está la muerte, sorda y segura, a nuestro lado los quince últimos días de la vida, y nosotros inocentes, disimulando, haciéndonos los distraídos, animados y hervidores de proyectos como si así pudiéramos escaparla. Pero esa afirmación tácita y suya no podía bastarle; se comprendía bien que era un engaño, y era menester que se lo dijeran, que alguien y no él le confirmara la esperanza. Desgraciadamente estaba solo. Los personajes de piedra esculpidos en los pilares tenían un secular hábito del silencio, y si alguno hablaba hacíalo por medio de una filacteria que saliéndole de la boca plantaba como un enhiesto banderín divino en el silencio, una muda frase latina, abstracta y desesperada del mundo. Se acercó a un rincón de la capilla del obispo. Una concha primorosamente tallada en la piedra tierna y rosácea de Hontoria le ofrecía carnosidades, casi color, de oreja humana. Dijo a media voz:

«Aún puede venir, apenas si son las seis.» Y ahora lo oyó, lo oyó muy bien, embelesado en sus mismas palabras. Narciso sin agua y con amante. Aquella esperanza que le rondaba por dentro se salió de su puro limbo, tomaba corporeidad en el sonido, y convertida gracias a aquel artificio, en materia, en vida sonora, avanzaba hacia él propia y ajena, ofreciéndole como una sorpresa el deseo mismo de su corazón. Pero hay voces, y ésta era una de ellas, con doble eco: uno afuera, en las rocas, en las paredes, que las repite tal como las queríamos, fidelísimo, y otro subrepticio, interior y extraño, con el que no contábamos, que deforma nuestras palabras y las devuelve sonando a todo lo contrario de lo que decían. Y entonces se comprende que aquella palabra de fuera, la que dimos al aire y vuelve del aire, es cosa falsa, hueca y vacía mentira, mientras que la verdad se alumbra silenciosa, revelándose a nosotros mismos, en ese eco interior, inaudito e inesperado. Y su: «Aún puede venir» rebotando en las cavernas del corazón le sonaba a desesperante: «Ya no vendrá, ya no vendrá». Soltó la esperanza, la dejó caer, como un tizón chispeante, maravilloso de ver a lo lejos, pero que ahora, cuando había ido a cogerle, le quemaba los dedos. Mejor dicho, la cambió por otra; acaso se había equivocado de hora e iba a venir exactamente retrasada a las siete. Sin embargo, él estaba seguro de que Matilde había dicho a las seis. Porque cuando ella escogió como una princesa que hunde la mano en un saquillo de perlas, de entre las veinticuatro horas del día, aquella hora irisada, mate, de las seis, recordaba Angel que esta cifra le sirvió a él, de pronto, para explicarse el mundo, que un momento antes, cuando no sabía si podría verla o no se le aparecía como un problema confuso e insoluble. El cielo limpio, encajonado entre dos filas de árboles, como un río, acarreaba hacia un mar desconocido flotantes y blanquísimas como leyendas, una, dos, tres, cuatro, cinco, seis, precisamente seis nubecillas de verano. La gran partida de ruleta crepuscular la ganaría de seguro un seis, allá en la casilla roja del horizonte donde iba a caer la bola, el sol seminublado y sin brillo. Y hasta la vida que corría azulada y sinuosa, por el brazo desnudo de Matilde, ensayaba sobre el blanquísimo fondo de su piel con escrituras de finas venas, un seis frustrado, incorrecto, pero inequívoco. No; no se había equivocado. La hora de la cita era las seis, y ya no vendría.

Pero, al fin y al cabo, ¿qué más le daba? Porque lo curioso estaba en que esa cita, esperada por él desde el día antes, no era con él. Si Matilde había quedado en venir a la catedral a las seis era por ver a Alfonso de Padilla. El día antes, hablando con sus amigas en el claustro de la Universidad, todas hicieron a Matilde grandes elogios del mancebo: de su cabellera larga y rizada, como de un paje, de las hazañas que se le atribuían, y de la mirada noble, fría y melancólica, digna de un caballero de otros tiempos. La mejor hora para verle era a las seis, en la catedral. Y entonces Matilde, que había escuchado en silencio, dijo firmemente, mirando derecha a Angel: «Mañana, a las seis, iré a la catedral». Y Angel se había introducido en aquella hora dulce y jugosa, como una fruta, todo agusanado y voraz, dispuesto a saborearla sin dejar nada a la otra boca a quien estaba ofrecida. ¿Qué importaba que no fuese para él? De todos modos vería a Matilde. Se estaría tendido al borde de la cita, acostado en la ribera de las seis, como se está a la orilla de un río que no fluye para nosotros, que va a otra cosa, pero que, sin embargo, al pasar, le arrancamos, furtivamente y sin tocarle, delicias exquisitas, sin más que verle correr hacia el mar. Por eso recorría la catedral enorme, solo.

Es decir, solo no, porque Alfonso de Padilla se encontraba en la iglesia desde mucho antes que Angel entrara. Por cierto que le sorprendió su actitud. Tenía en la mano derecha un libro abierto, pero sin leer, con un ademán vacío e inútil, de esos que sobreviven a las acciones, que perduran cuando ya se marchó su alma, la voluntad de ejecutarlas, dejando tras sí un espacio imposible de llenar con el ademán mismo, igual que ese hueco blanquísimo y suave que queda en el aire de la tarde cuando han pasado unas palomas. Y el libro manaba una tristeza de alcándara sin pájaro, porque la mirada que un momento antes descansaba en él, doble, negra y buida como unas garras, se le había escapado ahora, en desconocido vuelo, a cazas de altanería, sin duda muy recónditas, porque no estaba el mirar fuera de los ojos, sino tornado hacia los adentros del mancebo, tras una presa que nadie podía ver. Probablemente para esperar mejor, se había reclinado, tendido casi, en la piedra, reposada la mejilla en la mano, con tan elegante desprendimiento de las cosas ambientes, que cuando el sacristán pasó por allí, hizo como que no le veía, intimidado por su señorío y cual si estuviese ya acostumbrado a postura tan poco respetuosa en un templo catedral. Y lo más sorprendente de todo es que ni siquiera se atrevió a ahuyentar aquel perro que, atravesado y dormido, con unas blancas lanas que a la luz crepuscular tenían raros reflejos marmóreos, estaba, fiel y emblemático, a los pies de Alfonso de Padilla.

Ya pronto iban a dar las siete. El sacristán con unas llaves tintineantes en la mano empezó a acosar a las últimas luces del día, rezagadas en las capillas laterales de la iglesia, y que al oírle asustadas, por miedo a quedarse encerradas toda la noche, allí a oscuras, se escaparon, saltando por los altos ventanales dejando la iglesia sombría. Jorge se encaminó a la salida, despacio, penosamente cargado con una esperanza muerta. Pero de pronto el cortinón de la puerta del fondo de la iglesia se alzó: por allí entraban desatados, alegres, como una jauría, un tropel de rayos de sol, dorados, rojos, leonados, aullantes, saltando todos alrededor de una figura encendida y gallarda de mujer, rubia y esbelta, que traía bajo el brazo un carcaj parecido a una sombrilla corta. Los árboles que se entrevieron un instante, fuera y en último término, antes de que la puerta se cerrara, no eran ya, trasmutados por la figura femenil a que servían de momentáneo fondo, humildes acacias municipales, el jardinillo de la plaza de la Catedral, sino una espesa selva de Argólida, que recorría ardorosa y virgen, esta Diana cazadora, toda extrañada de haber dado en medio de ella con un edificio raro y de bárbaras proporciones, con una catedral gótica. El sacristán la reconoció en seguida, como a una diosa pagana, y aterrorizado de su audacia lanzó, por única defensa, su profesional anatema: «¡Que se va a cerrar, que se va a cerrar!», acompañado de un gran sonar de llaves. Ya la cortina estaba otra vez caída, y con ello los canes de la diosa, dorada escolta del crepúsculo, desaparecidos. Diana se quedó parada, sin paso, sin voz, sin alma, ante una edad nueva. Y entonces, perversa y femenina, con su poder divino, en una hábil metamorfosis no ovidiana, tomó la apariencia respetuosa y tímida de una señorita que llega tarde a la catedral, la figura misma, los rasgos exactos de Matilde. Angel la saludaba.

«Llego muy retrasada, ¿verdad?, qué pena. No podré verle.»

Salieron juntos, perseguidos, echados como de un frustrado paraíso, por las llaves y el paso del sacristán. Pero Angel sentía un placer satánico y secreto, porque él se marchaba con Matilde, andando a su lado, de carne y hueso, por una tarde palpitante y verdadera, mientras que su bello rival aborrecible, Alfonso de Padilla, señor de Olmos Albos, paje de la reina Católica, muerto en un romance fronterizo, frente a la Vega de Granada, se quedaría encerrado en la iglesia, a la sombra de un florido dosel de piedra, en su sepulcro gótico, deshecha ya la cita de los tres.

Delirios del chopo y el ciprés

A Mercedes y María Salvador, recordadas entre sus chopos de Burgos.

Introduccción. Cuando se pasaba en el tren, la mirada, ociosa en vacaciones, se prendía en aquellos dos árboles plantados en la comba más profunda del horizonte, señeros e iguales, tan el uno del otro, como los dos palos de una inmensa hache frustrada. Sacudíase la entredormida atención del ánimo, y picada por infantil prisa y diligencia, se precipitaba a sus deberes, y, dejando el tren, escalaba repechos, abreviaba atajos, saltaba cárcavas y, ya en el horizonte remoto, se convencía por minuciosos testimonios de visión y palpo de que aquellos dos árboles tan iguales eran un chopo y un ciprés. Volvía aceleradamente a la estación próxima, en donde el tren se había quedado aguardando, y sentado en la soledad inspiradora del departamento, tan perfectamente equilibrada por las compañías fugaces y alusivas de los paisajes laterales, escribía en su cuaderno americano: «Aforismo para mañana: A lo lejos, iguales; a lo cerca, tan paralelos, que nunca se encontrarán». La letra le salía temblona, séase por la emoción que manaba del hallazgo o por el movedizo asiento que ofrece cualquier convoy rodante al más seguro aforista.

Chopo. Anoche, bajo el cóncavo cuchicheo estelar, estuviste, confiésamelo, contento de tu destino y hasta recreado unas horas en profunda y lustral inmovilidad. Pero a la primer alba salta el primer viento, y otra vez te arrojas al atormentado tanteo de perfiles móviles sobre quietos horizontes, de siluetas destrenzadas en su misma inicial intención de vivir, todo lleno, rebosado, ahogado en tu forma del minuto por la afluencia de tantas formas en tu entraña que ya quieren ensayarse. Si cien veces te haces, cien te deshaces, y vives como la cadena, del eslabón de antes, del eslabón de después. Poca fama tienes en el contorno, pobre chopo, y con tu manoteo frenético, no pasarás de ser un sembrador de intenciones en este decidido páramo castellano que sabe lo que se hace. Porque nunca se aparta de ti ese ángel taimado y equívoco que te sopla en las orejillas el peligroso aviso de que tu forma no se

81

acertará sino en la torturada sucesión de las infinitas deformaciones.

Ciprés. Nadie te ha visto aprender, de cortos que fueron tus aprendizajes. Raíz certera, hincada en tierra apenas y que da ya con el jugo de la soterrada disciplina. Con hidalgo señorío de la forma lograda, tu empeño vital se concentra en la fiera y confiada insistencia de un recto perfil sobre blandos paisajes azules o escabrosos cielos atormentados. Y cuando viene el día te encuentra, y cuando viene la noche te encuentra, afanado en la labra paciente de tu escultura, acechando los consejos únicos de tu propia sombra de sol o luna por el suelo.

Chopo, agua. Cada paisaje baila al son que le hace su agua, mar, río, arroyo. Pero Castilla de estío, ¿dónde tiene—con los mares remotos, los cauces sin caudales, las sierras sin nieve—el agua de su vida sino en esta húmeda e incansable movilidad de chopos, en el vasto oleaje de las choperas a lo lejos, en ese burbujeo estremecido de los follajes y en esa gota seca, hoja del chopo, con que la tarde de viento nos salpica? Y ríos y mares ilusorios hacen danzar sus aguas detrás de este antifaz justo y transparente que le pone al paisaje un crepúsculo seco de Castilla.

Anécdota incidental. Llevábamos ocho días de recorrer por único campo las asfaltadas praderas de la ciudad, y sólo nos reposaban las luminosas sombras de las farolas, con su maravilloso follaje nocturno. Y como sentías nostalgia del suelo y los chopos de Castilla, te llevé al Museo. Tampoco allí pisaste tierra, sino pulidas maderas, de las que el olor de aguarrás te fingía trasuntos vagos de extraños campos de hierba con perfume penetrante y artificial, en haciendas australianas. No viste cielos; en su lugar, sabias cristalerías donde se templan y desbravan las luces de los fogosos días. Y ningún horizonte más que las cuatro paredes agujereadas por los ventanillos de los cuadros, en algunos de los cuales se habían olvidado de poner cristal y podía uno asomarse al asunto con medio cuerpo fuera. Te llevé a la sala de retratos, y allí, en los ojillos de un personaje desconocido (traje negro, barba lacia, color terrosa), estaba tu árbol de Castilla, alma tímida y vacilante, amorosa y llorosa como chopo de verano recién llovido, trémula toda ante esto y aquello, luz, aire, humo, chopo. Tú, por broma, escribiste en el catálogo: «Identificado este retrato de desconocido, por el Greco. Retrato de chopo con vagos accesorios fisonómicos e indumentarios. Pase a la sala de paisajes».

Chopo, otoño. ¡Rebullicios de plata, fervores de oro, pompas de mayo, orgullo de octubre, adiós, adiós! Azuza el viento de invierno a las dolorosas penitencias, y por los viales de Castilla los chopos desnudos se contorsionan con secos chasquidos de esqueletos mondos, para flagelarse los blancos huesos, miserias finales. Por el suelo van huidas, locas de persecución y de agonía, acosadas por las ascéticas jaurías del cierzo, las últimas sensualidades, doradas hojas secas.

Ciprés, ante la muerte. El ciprés es una decisión irrevocable de salvarse. Ni un solo día se apartó de la meta celeste esa voluntad suya corporeizada en el ahilado impulso de una silueta inquebrantable; y su sayal, nunca mudado, raído y pardo de lluvias, solaneras, vendavales y años, brinda la mejor vestidura al desprendimiento. En esta noche de neblina, que es una gran semejanza a la muerte, que es un borde de la muerte, ya se le ve al ciprés, ahuesado y ahusado, ese blancor largo e incorpóreo de las figuraciones, con que se representan en los cuadros las almas que, rozadas por las manos de dos ángeles, ascienden a los cielos merecidos.

Chopo, madera de cruz. Si no mueres por todos, tú sufres por todos. Ni la nube aplomada en el cielo, ni el sabueso dormido en la yacija, ni los ricitos volanderos quietos en las nucas de las muchachas, ni las campanas ahorcadas en las espadañas, nadie, nadie siente ese enemigo, sutil vientecillo que pasa por el aire, nadie se estremece ni se sacrifica. Con tus minutísimas hojas, contigo, chopo, sólo choca, y mientras la tarde entera se salva de inquietudes por torpe, por sorda, por baja, tú, centinela de todos, defiendes en la aparente calma total el desesperado deber de las ansias delicadas.

Aurora de verdad

Las citas con Aurora eran siempre por la mañana, porque entonces el día recientísimo y apenas usado es todo blanco y ancho, como un magnífico papel de cartas donde aún no hemos escrito más que la fecha y en cuyas cuatro carillas podremos volcar todas las atropelladas efervescencias del corazón sin que haya que apretar la letra más que un poco, al final, anochecido, cuando siempre falta espacio. Como la hora señalada eran las diez, Jorge se despertaba a las ocho y media. Lo primero que se encontraba, allí a su lado, enorme e impalpable, era la ausencia de Aurora. Ausencia por un momento inexplicable, ya que su amada estuvo toda la noche junto a él, más efusiva y cariñosa que nunca y no había motivo para que ahora, precisamente al abrir los ojos, dejara de verla, para que aquella conversación, recién iniciada, sobre un tema apasionante (pero imposible ahora, despierto, de recordar) se quedara así, empezada y cautivadora, como un periplo conservado en un palimpsesto incompleto. Saltaba de su cama, estrecha y unipersonal, e iba derecho a la mesa de escritorio, con aquella manía suya de anotarlo todo, para apuntar el primer adverso acontecimiento del día: «A las ocho y media, pérdida de Aurora». Pero al llegar frente al cuaderno dietario, antes de coger la pluma le saltaba a la vista la última frase escrita la noche anterior: «Mañana a las diez, cita con Aurora». Y ante el descubrimiento de que ese mañana de anoche estaba ya logrado y maduro, como una ciruela en su rama, colgado de los árboles del *square*, balanceándose sin prisa en el cielo, de que ese mañana era hoy, la tranquilidad renacía con la conciencia, y Aurora, como uno de esos objetos que se nos caen de las manos, pero que logramos atrapar antes de que lleguen al suelo, parecía sin haberse realmente perdido. Abría el balcón, miraba el reloj, en busca de corroboraciones. Entre la Aurora del sueño irreal y discursiva, recién abandonada entre las sábanas, a la otra verdadera y silenciosa que iba a encontrar muy pronto en el Museo, corrían como entre dos orillas gemelas y separadas, noventa minutos, hora y media, lentas aguas.
Jorge no se paraba a mirar melancólicamente a aquella ribera distante aún y deseada, sino que, alegre y provechosamente, con

el baño, con vestirse y desayunar, suprimía distancias. A las nueve y media estaba en la calle. Y aunque la reunión con Aurora era para treinta minutos más tarde, en cuanto salía al bulevar empezaba ya a encontrársela. Porque no hallaba a Aurora de pronto, de una vez, por súbita aparición ante la vista, sino poco a poco, por lentos avances, como da el filósofo con la verdad, a fuerza de elaboraciones interiores prendidas en severos datos reales. En el asfalto, por el suelo, lo primero que veía era' la sombra de una modistilla transeúnte, sombra exactamente parecida a aquella Aurora, cuando el día anterior, yendo los dos por el Parque, se inclinó Jorge a recoger el abanico, que se la había caído, y tropezó, allí detrás, en la arena dorado con una Aurora compendiada y exacta, azul y vagamente deformada como una imagen en el fondo del estanque. Ya, apenas salido a la calle, tenía de otra, pero tan suya, la sombra de Aurora. Y en seguida, a cada paso se encontraba con más cosas de ella. Porque aunque era única e inconfundible estaba, sin embargo, en todas partes, fluida, preciosa y desaprovechada, como un agua sin forma. Precisamente aquella dama alta y seca, que cruzaba en aquel momento la plaza, llevaba un sombrerito de paja de Italia como el que ella se había traído, y puesto un día con cierto rubor de turista romántica, de su último viaje a Florencia. Seguía Jorge muy contento de haber espigado, en tan breve espacio, dos fragmentos de su amor completo, una sombra y una cofia de paja; y de pronto en la plataforma de un tranvía que pasaba salpicando a todo el mundo de atención y campanilleos iba una muchacha—invisible el rostro, vuelto hacia el otro lado—, pero que para guardar el equilibrio tomó una postura de torcido reposo, de atormentada estabilidad, igual a la que ensayaba Aurora una tarde, en el barco, sobre las movidas aguas del Canal para darle una idea de cierta línea exquisita y difícil de una escultura de Estrasburgo. Un poco más allá, veía a una joven que, a pesar de su honesta apariencia, llevaba pendiente del cuello a modo de un precioso colgante, triangular y rosado, y cual si fuese suyo, el descote de Aurora. Y por una calle afluente al bulevar, distante y de lado, como una idea complementaria, llegaba la ondulación suave del Mediterráneo, herido por el viento, como si aquella blusilla azul y levísima que temblaba a cualquier soplo, aquella blusilla de Aurora, tan aficionada a cambiar de trajes, la hubiese tirado anoche al mar su amiga.

Poco a poco la figura aún invisible y distante se formaba por la coincidencia de aquellos abigarrados elementos exteriores que la ciudad le ofrecía sueltos, incoherentes, pero que él, gracias al modelo, a la imagen ejemplar que llevaba grabada en el corazón, iba colocando cada uno en su sitio igual que las piezas de un *puzzle*. Y ya faltaban muy pocas, porque como la ciudad era tan animada y abierta, con perspectivas hondas de mar y de montaña, tan rica de tráfico y abundantísima en razas y variedades indumentarias, formas, líneas, colores de todas clases le salían al paso copiosamente, quietas y embalsamadas unas, como las frutas, los rebrillos de alhajas y los visos de las telas, tras los cristales de los escaparates, vertiginosas e indecisas otras, trajes, rostros de unos oficiales árabes, que cruzaban a toda velocidad en un automóvil, algunas, las más infelices, sujetas y atormentadas por su liberación en verdes manoteos de árboles, detrás de las verjas de los parques y las más venturosas, libres y sin dueño, girovagas en el aire matinal, jirones de nubes, vilanos. Y sin embargo, a pesar de aquella opulencia de recursos y a pesar, sobre todo, de lo claro que estaba el original deseado en su corazón, Jorge no podía encontrarse realmente con Aurora entera y cabal hasta que la tuviera delante, porque siempre le faltaban unas cuantas cosas esenciales, huecos que no podría llenar mientras que ella con su primer saludo no le diera, en la sencilla fórmula del «Buenos días», aquellas tres piezas únicas e insustituibles: mirada, sonrisa y voz.

Ya se iba acercando al Museo, llevando aquella figura descabalada, una estatuilla deliciosa e incompleta a la que había que poner ojos, dibujar labios e infundir palabra, hacerla obra vivificada y perfecta, cosa que no lograría sino con la colaboración de Aurora, colaboración fácil, y sin pena, simple presencia. Subió las escaleras del Museo y, como siempre, el portero le llamó para advertirle que se había olvidado de dejar el bastón. Era muy temprano y no había más público que el compuesto por todos esos personajes insignificantes y menores de los cuadros holandeses que se pasan todo el día, inmóviles y admirativos, vigilados por los guardianes, sin duda por no ser gente de confianza, en el Museo, para ver de cerca y detenidamente a tanto príncipe y señor engolado y solemne, de los retratados por Tiziano y Rubens. Aurora y Jorge habían convenido en citarse cada día en una sala distinta, por orden estrictamente cronológico, lo cual si tenía el inconveniente de parecer a primera vista escolarmente pedantesco, ofrecía a Aurora un fondo cambiante y siempre bellísimo, de acentuada progresión hacia la luz y el color, haciéndola pasar por delicadas transiciones, del ambiente de rocas, torpe y seco de Giotto, a las flores de Renoir, de una concepción del mundo teatral y enfática al modo veneciano, a esta liberalidad alegre, jugosa y semidesnuda, de los paisajes con ninfas, pintados hace diez años.

Llevaban casi un mes de verse, y aquel día la sala de reunión era la de Turner. Así que Aurora sería el único ser vivo poblador de aquel paraíso ultraterrenal, la Eva creada al revés, antes que el hombre y esperándole en un mundo recién inventado, vago, cálido y palpitante aún, y que tenía por árbol de la ciencia un espléndido pino de Italia. Empujó la pesada puerta y sintió en seguida la atmósfera densa y caliente, de treinta y cinco grados, de aquella pintura. Eva, Aurora, no estaba, la creación se había retrasado; y Jorge comenzó a pasear por aquel cosmos grandiosamente elemental, donde el aire, el agua y la tierra no se diferenciaban bien unos de otros porque Dios acababa de separarlos, un deseo de Aurora, un afán primigenio y adánico de la mujer compañera. Desdeñoso de los cuadros en torno, se volvió hacia su imaginación, donde la veía, a ella casi completa, tocada, vestida, calzada con aquellas impalpables prendas espigadas en el camino y el recuerdo. Sí, así era: iba a llegar, en realidad, pero estaba ahora tan familiar, allí dentro tan parecida, hecha casi por él, que su aparición no le sorprendería sino como la última inspiración felicísima que da remate a un poema trabajado mucho tiempo y que ya se sabe casi de memoria. Se acercó al ancho balcón que daba a los muelles; precisamente en aquel instante se escapaba del campo visual desde allí dominado, viniendo hacia acá, como para entrar en el Museo, una figura femenina, que apenas si pudo entrever, pero que así en fugaz mancha con su sombrero pajizo, su corpiño azul, su rosado descote respondía a la imagen interior de Aurora trazada por Jorge sobre su imagen real de la víspera. Sí, ella tenía que ser. Pero mientras Jorge inclinaba su última duda sobre la silueta fugitiva y perdida, Aurora sin que él la sintiera, había entrado en la sala. «Vengo un poco tarde, ¿verdad?» Retumbaron las palabras por encima de aquellos paisajes desiertos, llegaron a Jorge amplificadas, prolongadas por el eco que suscitaron en un «Amanecer entre rocas» que había colgado a la izquierda. Se volvió, y al verla, un asombro inmenso le sobrecogía. Porque Aurora llevaba un sombrerito obscuro de gamuza, traje gris y sin descote, y se acercaba ella sola, sin la sombra azulada de ayer, de hace un momento en la calle. La creación fidelísima, de la mañana y el pensamiento, la figura inventada y esperada se venía abajo de un golpe, porque Jorge la había labrado con lo conocido, con los datos de ayer, con el pasado. Y lo que tenía delante, intacta y novísima, en la virginal pureza del paraíso, tendiéndole la mano, contra costumbre sin guante, era la vida de hoy, era Aurora de verdad.

Volverla a ver

Al asomarme al balcón del hotel, estrenando la luz de la mañana, a aquel balcón que dominaba el caserío y el puerto, la tierra que me sostenía, el mar que a ella me trajo, y muy al fondo la sigilosa línea embozada de la costa de Europa, de donde vine y donde nací, a aquel balcón que daba a sutiles bosquecillos blancos, crestas de olas, a ondulación marina y verdosa de pinares, al trabajo y al ocio, a Dios y a los hombres, casi a una perfecta síntesis filosófica y autobiográfica de mis veintitrés años, lo primero que vi, lo único que vi, fue su nombre. Había llovido la noche anterior, de modo que estaba limpio, legible, brillante como una decisión de espíritu sencillo. Calculaba yo: «Las letras deben de tener por lo menos veinte metros, porque desde aquí, y estoy lejos, se leen muy bien». Y paseaba sensualmente la vista por los enormes caracteres refiriéndolos con deleitosa complacencia a la persona de carne y hueso a que aludían. La *L* firme y precisa, como su silueta en marcha, y ahora inmóvil. La *X* con sus dos aspas, tan parecidas a aquellos dos caprichos suyos, contradictorios, de una tarde, cruzados; a una cosa que quiso primero y después desdeñó porque quería la que dejaba por aquella, y yo vi muy claro que en el fondo eran ambas las deseadas, así, juntas y contrarias, como en la letra, las dos. La *S* semejante a sus bromas, sinuosas y rematadas con refinada perfección, pero a veces tan secas, tan inquietantes que parecían una *Z*. De la *B* me apartaba a toda prisa, fugitivo de su vista, de la envuelta indicación pareja de un pecho firme y momentáneamente eterno, sin respiro. La *Y* me empapó todo, como un rocío, del recuerdo de una tarde en el tenis, cuando su enigmático carácter, sostenido en su grácil cuerpo, se sostenía, tendido y esforzado, en la blanca punta del pie, cual si anduviera por invisible cuerda echada de la tarde a la noche, sobre el rojizo abismo del crepúsculo. Pero en ninguna me detenía tanto como en esa deliciosa *V*, discreta muestra de su corazón, estilizada oferta del bien más puro y deseado, noble corazón que estaba todo el día en el tejado, mirando al cielo. Cuando las nubes volanderas jugaban a tapar y destapar con el sol, luces y sombras, cayendo sobre la *V* en fingidas sístoles y diástoles luminosas, la animaban con una vida embriagadora y falsa, y parecía que mi sangre marchaba al compás marcado por aquel inhumano, óptico latido. Hasta el punto, que meticulosamente cerraba el nombre, fuera ya de él, despidiendo de él, pero todavía suyo, me recordaba las despedidas, el adiós final, redondo y rodado con que ella al mismo tiempo que me alejaba de su presencia me tendía ya el cabo del recuerdo. Se me cansaron los ojos de fijarme tanto en el nombre trazado con gigantescas letras negras sobre el rojo tejado del gran depósito de la casa, en el muelle. Había que apartarlos de allí.

Precisamente, como si hubiera oído mi antojo de otra cosa y la misma, un barco entraba en el puerto, delicadamente colgado de las azules bambalinas celestes por un leve hilo de humo, tan leve y casi invisible, que parecía que el barco marchaba solo. Por afán de distracción cogí los gemelos, me acerqué el vapor a los ojos, y fui a poner la vista en el nombre del navío. Y ¡oh maravilla! las mismas letras tendidas al sol, en el tejado, reposadas e indelebles a la sombra constante de mi pensamiento, eran las que se ostentaban pintadas todas de blanco, como sus trajes estivales de yacht-woman, en los costados de aquel vapor, de aquella aparición. Las olas corrían apresuradamente a humillarse con espumeante alegría, una tras otra, ante sus pies, como cumplidos fáciles y monótonos. Y un cortejo de gaviotas que revoloteaba insistentemente sobre el barco no dudé que iba acechando la más propicia ocasión para caer sobre aquellos caracteres y llevarse cada cual su letra en el pico, tesoro precioso eternamente disperso, diamantes sin sentido separados de la joya perfecta por inhábiles ladrones. El nombre iba entrando majestuosamente en la rada. Le saludaron, con sus desgarrados pañuelos, dos o tres sirenas, en bienvenida. Un remolcador se precipitó oficiosamente a su encuentro cumpliendo papel de criado que al detenerse el coche despliega el estribo donde se va a posar el pie de su señora. Luego el nombre dio unas vueltas, se paró; y para estarse tan quieto y legible como el del tejado sólo le sobraba el leve balanceo del puerto, última coquetería del mar, recuerdo complacido de la travesía en el reposo. Iba a dejar los gemelos cuando en alto mástil vi una banderola chillona y estremecida de brisa, con algo, temblando, escrito en ella. No, no era su nombre. Demasiado grande, muchas letras, para subirlas a todas tan arriba. A nadie se le ocurre que llegaremos a los cielos con las vestiduras y alhajas que en el mundo consideramos indispensables, sino purificados, hechos compendio, vueltos alma. Así ella escrita en los azules cielos matinales ascendía hasta allí tras la previa depuración de su nombre en dos iniciales, *P. B.*, incompleta y esencial, y la blanca banderola marcaba con dos letras rojas su triunfo definitivo, la posesión celeste.

Exquisita delicia ésta de volverse de espaldas al alma para pensar en ella, de tener que abrir, los ojos, en avizorante atención a lo exterior, en lugar de cerrarlos melancólicamente, buscadores de íntimas contemplaciones. Para recordarla no había que tocar sutiles resortes mentales que dieran suelta a evocaciones secretas; bastaba con el ejercicio puro y simplicísimo de un sentido corporal, con pasear la mirada por tierra, mar y cielos, seguro de encontrarla doquiera, alegre y cosquilleada la nuca por el viento, en las banderolas, grave y perezosa en el tejado, y aún temblorosa, húmeda, llorada, en blancos reflejos, cuando se duplicaban deformadamente en el agua de la rada las blancas letras pintadas en los lados del vapor. Todos los ámbitos de la vida, espacios surcados por quillas, alas o plantas, tenían su marca y señal, cantarines de la gloria y poderío de una criatura sobre el mundo. Y de pronto, al traer la mirada más cerca, al amplio bulevar que estaba a mis pies, vi que un camión enorme y gris se llevaba a toda prisa, con alegres mugidos de toro raptor, su nombre, pintado de azul. Lo llevaría por la ciudad y los campos, para que ojos atónitos lo deletrearan rápidamente, sin comprender su significado, como una escritura fugaz y sagrada; lo pasearía orgullosamente indiferente como el pendón de un conquistador en la recién ganada villa. Ya rendido de tanta presencia cerré los ojos, para no pensar en ella. Pero también estaba aquí a este lado, dentro, escrita al revés como una página copiada en un espejo, que al principio no se ve clara, pero que se entiende en seguida en cuanto se la lea a la inversa, empezando por la izquierda del corazón.

Me puse a distraerme, a huir de ella, leí un rato, fui a las librerías, compré papel de escribir de muchas clases escogiendo minuciosamente, me paré ante una cartelera, leyendo con atención los anuncios de unos espectáculos repulsivos; compuse, en suma, una hora artificial y fingida, encarnizadamente, como se compone por capricho y distracción un poemita latino, pero que luego resulta acróstico porque sin querer empezamos cada verso con una de esas letras que tan grabadas tenemos en un orden dado y que precisamente queríamos olvidar con tal entretenimiento. Desesperado volví al hotel, entré furtivamente en el ascensor, en mi cuarto, en la cama. De pronto el timbre del teléfono dio un brusco tirón del silencio, le volteó como una ancha campana.

«Preguntan por el señor.»

«¿Quién; qué nombre?»

Y con los ojos cerrados, como los cierra el reo ante los fusiles del pelotón que le va a quitar la vida, para no ver lo que es seguro, aquello de que no escapará, esperé yo que ascendiera, dicho, cantado, exaltado hasta aquel quinto piso por la voz ronca del portero aquel nombre—MISS PRISCILLA BEEXLEY—que me iba derecho allí donde ya estaba, al corazón.

Contra mi costumbre pedí el ascensor. Tardó. No subía, acaso no subiría nunca, quizá el timbre que yo acababa de oprimir se había estropeado e iba yo a estarme allí en el descansillo, a veinticinco metros de Miss Beexley, incomunicado con ella para siempre, suspendido en el espacio intermedio y mostrenco de un rellano de escalera, entre el cielo y la tierra, como un ángel castigado de Dios. Porque claro es que no había que pensar en el otro camino, en bajar hasta ella de escalón en escalón. Así se iba a todas las cosas sólitas y sin importancia, al museo, al club, al embarcadero, a Europa, a América, a lo desconocido. Pero yo no me dirigía en el presente momento a paraje identificable en norte o sur, en capricho o desesperación, sino a un lugar que sólo tiene acceso por una inmersión súbita y decisiva, por una caída tan impuesta y voluntariosa, simultáneamente, que la fuerza de gravedad que nos arrastra se antoja ejercicio desembarazado y libre, graciosa atribución humana. La voluntad estaba tan empeñada en una cosa, que no podía convertirse en motriz de ningún miembro corpóreo, porque toda su fuerza la aplicaba a querer, a querer en la inmovilidad. Por eso la escalera era imposible, y allí donde yo iba requeríase marchar con los ojos cerrados, quieto, rígido, como las momias egipcias marchan, en una dirección precisamente opuesta, solemnes y perfumadas, en el momentáneo ataúd del ascensor. Y aun marchar, ir, no son palabras justas. Hundirse, como la esponja, que a medida que desciende se precipita más porque su misma caída, agua, peso, la empapa de acelerada prisa en caer. Así yo había de hundirme hasta una arena fina sembrada de horas complicadas y fragilísimas como corales, de floraciones intrincadas y mal definidas, tipos de algas que no se ha llegado a catalogar, de conchas cerradas o entreabiertas, deliciosamente irisadas y todas sin perla. Arena dormida bajo capa de tiempo. Porque donde yo iba era al pasado, al pasado de Priscilla y mío; iba después de tres años, por vez primera, a volverla a ver.

Repentino, sordo y encendido como la llama saltó delante de mí el ascensor, abriéndome su corazón asalariado. No tuve que dar más que un paso, adentro. Y la vida comenzó a correr, vertiginosamente al revés. Se deshacía el tiempo, conforme lo atravesaba el ascensor. Al cruzar por cada piso se leían como en una columna de termómetro, las distancias aniquiladas. Los tres años que de Priscilla me separaban al comenzar, eran sólo dos frente al segundo piso, apenas unos meses al cruzar por delante de la esmerilada puerta del entresuelo, y se reducían milagrosamente a semanas, a días, a horas, con rapidez exactamente paralela a la del descenso, conforme nos acercábamos a tierra. Y cuando, ya abajo, el criado alzó la cortina tendida ante la puerta del salón donde Priscilla esperaba, me encontré con que los tres años de vida en ausencia estaban completamente desvividos y que este día de volverla a ver era, abolición perfecta y sin rastro de los tiempos intermedios, el día mismo que nos despedimos.

Livia Schubert, incompleta

Está escrita la hora de mi infelicidad. Ni un minuto antes ni un minuto después: seré desgraciado puntualmente esta noche, a la una y treinta y cinco. En la Edad Media las suertes y las desdichas las escriben, con pluma de ave, sobre un pergamino terso y celestial, adobado por soles y lluvias, las cornejas, cuyo vuelo caprichoso decide, diestro o siniestro, los destinos. Hoy es más fácil: el sino, por lo menos mi sino, está al alcance de la mano, anda impreso en tirada copiosísima de un libro vulgar, y puede buscarse en el índice alfabético recorriendo vertiginosamente la escala de nombres y números, igual que se recorre un teclado en busca de una nota—¿cuál?: ¿do, re, fa?—con la punta del dedo y apoyada aquí, en su carne, el corazón. Ya está: página 223. Hermosa página, soberbia literatura evocadora de tierras bellísimas e incógnitas en un lenguaje sobrio y penetrante, sin un solo adjetivo, y tan ansioso de precisión, que, agotadas las posibilidades verbales, salta de las letras a los números y se expresa como la poesía superior, la matemática, en cifras. Nada inútil; ni una partícula, ni una rima. ¿Prosa o poesía? No se sabe. Palabras desnudas y puras, ordenadas, aquí en el centro, unas debajo de otras como los versos, parecidas de lejos a versos o a ondas, todas distintas, pero apoyadas en la siguiente, y que van a la misma cosa. Y luego, a derecha e izquierda, como dos orillas exactas y firmísimas de tierra, de dos y dos son cuatro, números, dos márgenes de números, viendo pasar ellos, lo inmutable, lo eterno, como dos filas de chopos, esa corriente cantarina de las palabras fugaces, por en medio. Toda esta composición extraña va encerrada en un recuadro negro, y lleva un título de poema modernísimo: *Itinerario,* 63. Mi infelicidad está escrita, no en el libro enorme y tan difícil de consultar del destino, sino en una guía de ferrocarriles, en el renglón que dice: «Lucéntum: llegada, una y treinta y dos; salida, una y treinta y cinco». Y no lleva mi desdicha uno de esos nombres pomposos y definitivos que la suelen poner las gentes—dolor, desesperación, desengaño, muerte—; se llama, sencillamente, expreso 22, París-Praga; todo afilado y de metal, como una saeta disparada eléctricamente por el arco tendido de la Gare du Nord, que irá a caer allá en Praga, Walisova, sin haber encontrado otro obstáculo en su camino que este blando corazón inesperado, el mío, que se puso en medio y será atravesado limpiamente, sin sangre, esta noche a la una y treinta y cinco, cuando cruce por el cielo de Lucéntum y se lleve entre sábanas a mi Livia Schubert, arrullándola como a un niño entredormido, con un son de hierro, para que no se acuerde de mí y coja el sueño pronto. En el fondo, no me disgusta que la desgracia sea puntual, precisada en el tiempo, separando la vida de la vida en un momento matemáticamente previsto e inexorable como una ejecución de pena de muerte. Nada de aquellas incertidumbres, cuando niño, esa vez que se anunció el fin del mundo, con toda garantía científica, para tal semana, y que me costó tantas noches sin dormir y una desilusión cruel, y este escepticismo sin remedio. No; esta vez el infortunio vendrá a su hora. Ya estará formado para salir; brillante, con las mesas del restaurán puestas y el humo preparado, recogida su fuerza para lanzarse toda a fondo con su enorme peso, en cuanto le impulse, redondo, tierno y breve, como un dedo infantil, el silbido del jefe de estación. Y ahora, a las seis, a la misma hora en que me encuentre por última vez con Livia, dentro de diez minutos, empezará a navegar rapidísima, por el cielo de la noche, a quinientos kilómetros de aquí, esa nube negra que tiene que descargar su rayo entre nosotros a la una y treinta y cinco, abriendo en la tierra una cárcava tan enorme de distancias, que nos quedemos, ella a un lado, yo al otro, separados por toda la vida.

Me despido de ella mientras duerme ese sueño de las seis de la tarde, ese sueño precipitado, corto y galopante como un Gran Premio de mil metros. La miro por última vez, me miro en ella por última vez. Porque estas coincidencias, ella y yo, Lucéntum, estío, sus labios, el día y la hora de la cita, su risa y mi felicidad, que han vivido juntas, pegadas unas a otras por espacio de dos meses, se van a separar en cuanto Livia, con su voz delgadísima, afilada aún más en el adiós, corte, inevitablemente y sin querer, el sartal que las enhilaba. Y ya me veo entonces, por muchos días, inclinado buscándolas, dispersas por el suelo, equivocándome a cada instante, creyendo que esta tarde, cristalina y transparente como un diamante, que veo delante de mí al doblar la esquina de las doce, es tarde de cita, que esta ciudad afanosa, de trescientos mil habitantes, sigue habitada, cuando en realidad su población, Livia Schubert y su alma, ha emigrado: se fue allá lejos, a dos mil kilómetros, como una reina perseguida, a plantar una villa nueva, a poblarla de gozo y de sonrisa, izando por encima de unos cielos con niebla, su alegre, su alegre pabellón invencible y colorinesco. Ahora, en este momento, todavía estoy en Livia, soy algo en ella: soy el desorden de su cuerpo dormido. Esa cabellera que se arrastra dorada y larguísima como un crepúsculo; esa mejilla derecha, pálida, mate, contrastando con la otra (yo estaba a la izquierda), encendida y arrebatada; esa asimetría en el desnudo, un seno oculto, descubierto el otro, que la da un aire de amazona yacente y vencedora: todo eso es mío, como es de la voz el eco. Hay algo más, mío también, pero no se puede ver, porque tiene los ojos cerrados; y aun si los abriera, no se vería, porque está en ellos caído y hondísimo, olvidado, igual que se olvida el agua de todo lo que echamos en ella, y que la conmueve tanto, que la agita en ondas dilatadas, pero luego se queda en el fondo, aplastado por una tersura sin inquietud. La cara de Livia apenas si se ve: tiene encima tantos besos precipitados y superpuestos, míos y más míos, tanta mirada posada y reposada en el mismo ámbito ovalado y breve que esas facciones que yo veo, sostenidas como en un supuesto indispensable en el semblante carnal de Livia, son el rostro de otra desesperada criatura, la cara de mi amor a Livia. Me miro vivo, despierto, en la patética vigilia de la despedida, en su faz dormida. Estoy en ella por última vez. Porque en cuanto Livia despierte empezará, lenta y minuciosa, mi destrucción, la ruina de mi efímera obra. Lo primero que se quitará Livia será la desnudez que yo la puse sobre el cuerpo. Y luego, frente al espejo, encarnizadamente, sin un descuido, irá, a fuerza de lociones, de crema, de lápices, arrojándome de su rostro, arrancando sin piedad, beso a beso, todo mi amor, que estaba allí cubriéndolo. Con una barrita roja se pintará encima de mis labios, que se quedaron allí en su boca, dobles, indelebles, con el último beso, otros labios terceros y artificiales. Y por fin blandirá, todo metálico y brillante, como un arma invencible, el peine de plata para desprenderse de esas pobres caricias enredadas, lo más conmovido y secreto de mi amor, que estaba allí, refugiado en los laberintos de cabello que yo le inventé. Y se quedará ante el espejo, yo deshecho, rehecha ella, convertida lo que era hace un instante rica y tumultuosa vida en mis brazos, en una biografía correctísima, sin una imperfección.

Porque esta imperfección que he sido yo, en su rostro, en su carne, estará ya borrada, como una arruga prematura y sin fuerza. No se llevará nada mío; no lo quiere, no lo quiso nunca. Es decir, se llevará lo mismo mío que trajo: mis tres libros, que se sabe casi de memoria, lo que pueden tener todos, y tal como lo tienen todos comprados, antes de conocerme, sin querer que la ponga ni siquiera mi firma en ellos, como si temiera que mi pluma, mi nombre, se marcara más allá del libro, en esa página de detrás: su alma, que ya no me pertenece y que está toda en blanco. De lo demás de esas tres horas, de todos los días, por espacio de mes y medio (tres horas iguales y sin repetirse nunca, unos días aquí, cuadradas, interiores, con un balcón que al llegar nos parece que da a la tarde, pero que luego, cuando nos marchamos, vemos que daba a la noche; tres horas, otras veces, panorámicas y sin dimensiones, que estaban arrolladas como una cinta en el paisaje, y que ella y yo, solos en el coche, desplegamos alegremente, dejándonoslas luego atrás, con sus bosques y sus castillos, su melancolía y su Edad Media, olvidadas, pasadas de prisa, como las descripciones de Walter Scott; tres horas, una tarde, ojivales, sin luz directa del cielo, iluminadas, como un misal, por un artista del siglo XIII, el auto de las vidrieras, sentados los dos en un banco de la catedral; tres horas, eso sólo una vez, con toldilla a rayas, y un nombre escrito a los dos lados: «Mon plaisir», que yo impulso aceleradamente, a ratos, con los remos, por el Rin, o dejo, cuando Livia me lo manda, flotar sobre la onda como una felicidad ligera y sin peso, que no se hundirá nunca y en la que nos hemos embarcado los dos), de todas estas tres horas no se llevará nada.

En el fondo, quizá lo hace por equidad, por un sentimiento de justicia, y no quiere nada mío porque ella no me deja tampoco cosa alguna. Mejor dicho, no quiere dejarme nada. Me ha dado eso que está ahí, dormido y de color de rosa, en el lecho. Y, cuando me lo dio, yo creí que era una prenda, una entrega simbólica y solemne, anticipo y compromiso de la donación total. Pero no me ha dejado pasar de ahí. Digo mal: para que yo no pasara de ahí, se ha puesto toda ella fuera, en el borde de su ser, en su cuerpo, y así, como una nación que tiene todos sus encantos en las ciudades de la frontera, ya no tengo motivo para ir más allá. Sería ridículo decir que me ha cerrado el paso a su alma. No; la ha puesto, generosamente, precipitada, encima de su carne, más desnuda que el cuerpo mismo, visible y sin misterio. Tanto, que ya no la veo, y al abrazarla, no siento otro contacto que el de su deliciosa, corpórea realidad. Entonces, mi insatisfacción, insatisfacción doctrinal y dogmática que viene de lejos, de la definición consagrada: «el hombre es un compuesto de cuerpo y alma», se ha puesto a trabajar, y yo la he fabricado un alma. A mi modo, como se reconstituye con unos cuantos vagos ademanes de mármol, desparramados por los museos y sin cabeza, una escena de la teogonía, la he hecho el alma de dentro, y la tengo aquí, hipotética y reconstituida, todo tembloroso de esta restauración de una obra de arte, cercana y perdida.

Sí; así tiene que ser. Me la oculta por pudor, por reserva, por altanería; no sé por qué. Pero yo, pacientemente, la he adivinado, y la tengo aquí, suya y mía, y me dejará, ella que no me quiere dejar nada, su alma, que es al mismo tiempo mi obra, entre las manos. ¡Qué bien, si me hubiera permitido probársela un día!

Este alma, hecha a la medida, con escrupuloso cuidado, que no ha omitido nada, ni la línea escurrida y esbelta de la cadera, ni el color variable de los ojos, ni la longitud un poco excesiva de la pantorrilla, estoy seguro de que se habría ajustado, impalpable y ceñidísima como un deseo, a su forma corporal. ¡Día feliz, día de Livia, sin falta, completa! Pero así, ¿qué voy a hacer? Tendré que quedarme con ese alma hecha sin encargo, y ella huída, con un alma hipotética y provisional, imposible de confrontar con la auténtica, y que acabará por ser, ella que es una realidad palpitante, a fuerza de no hallar apoyo en ningún cuerpo, una creación de mi fantasía, una obra literaria. ¡Si pudiera ensayarla, ahora que está dormida, por sorpresa! Aunque ella no se enterara, tan sólo por no quedarme con esa duda clavada de si «sería así . . .» Pero no va a ser posible. Habría que moverla un poco, probar si entra bien en el alma del brazo que yo hice ese brazo, largo y rosado, que está caprichosamente tendido en la almohada, y sobre todo alzar los párpados y ver si encajan en esas órbitas, los dos ojos del alma, mía, de Livia, la parte más delicada y primorosa de mi trabajo, la obra maestra de mi reconstitución. No es posible: entre su alma original, dormida dentro de un sueño, y esta réplica exactísima y emocionada que yo traigo, está infranqueable, rendido, inerte, un cuerpo, resistencia suprema, porque se me acaba de entregar.

De pronto se agita, como el cielo a la primera brisa del día, imperceptiblemente, porque la acaricia sin duda un vientecillo del despertar; habla, dice algo. Me acerco ansiosamente. Tengo el presentimiento de que su alma, ahora que ella está ausente y abandonada, se va a asomar, como una cautiva de romance cuando se aleja el moro guardián, aquí a los labios, haciendo posible la confrontación. Me acerco, llevando en la mano el alma de mi hechura, para ver si así se encuentran, iguales, en un alma única, suya y mía, definitiva. Pero no. El cuerpo vuelve, apenas estremecido, a su reposo. Y las dos palabras que sonriente se la escaparon de los labios, en vez de aclararlo todo, lo entenebrecen todo. Porque son dos palabras extrañísimas: mi nombre, Melchor, y unido a él por primera vez en la vida, otro nombre desconocido: Susana. Dijo: «Melchor, Susana». Me retiro derrotado, vacilante. Este dato nuevo, Susana, que por lo visto está anclado en el fondo de su vida, lo descompone todo. Habrá que rehacer el alma, contando ahora con él. ¿Pero quién es él, ella, Susana? No me da tiempo siquiera a preguntarlo, porque Livia se despierta. La luz, como una chiquilla que aprovecha cualquier descuido para irse a jugar a la calle, se ha ido, mientras mi distracción, afuera. Es ya de noche. Y por un momento, hasta que Livia da con el botón de la electricidad, no hay aquí en el cuarto, lo mismo exactamente que en mi alma, otra claridad que el blanco resplandor de su cuerpo desnudo.

Estaba aquí escondido, agazapado en el rincón más secreto de mi corazón, el deseo, todo tembloroso, de ir a la estación con Livia, de verla marchar; deseo avergonzado que no se atreverá a asomarse, ni siquiera a los ojos, porque conoce muy bien el horror que ella tiene a las escenas sentimentales y a los gestos definitivos. Y esto es lo insólito, la sorpresa de la despedida: que Livia se entra desenvuelta por mi pecho, llega sedosa y certera, igual que un hurón a esa guarida donde está mi deseo, y cogiendo esa bestezuela tímida y asustada, me la trae ella en la boca, en los labios, en la palabra, ofreciéndomelo a mí que lo crié, como si fuese un deseo suyo.

«Quiero que vengas a la estación.»

Y toda la noche, envuelta, más que en la negrura nocturna, en la honda tiniebla de la despedida, se ilumina, no con una luz difusa y amorfa, vagamente aclaratoria y romántica como la de la luna, sino con unas luces recortadas, concretas, hechas palabras dotadas de esa poesía estricta y sorprendente del anuncio luminoso: «Quiero que vengas a la estación». Yo propongo tímidamente ir a buscarla a su casa; pero ella, firme y sonriente, me corrige:

«No, mejor será que vayamos separados. El tren sale a treinta y cinco, de modo que puedes venir a las . . .»

Livia vacila, duda, se interrumpe. Y no sólo se detiene el hilo de la voz en sus labios, el latido de mi corazón, sino que veo que todo en torno mío, obedece, en una pausa cósmica, y se para pendiente de lo que Livia vaya a decir. Frenan chirriantes los automóviles; un ómnibus immenso a poco se estrella contra la esquina; el negro del *jazz-band* del café Inglés, en la terraza, se queda con la boca abierta y el alarido colgando en el aire, y el reloj municipal se retrasa, parado, exactamente lo que ella tarda en hablar, quince segundos.

«Bueno . . . , puedes venir . . . un momento antes.»

Se reanuda el tráfico, vibran los motores, rueda el mundo, y el grito del cantante se clava, agudo, como un alfiler de cabeza negra, en la almohadilla mullida y azul del cielo de septiembre. Y Livia desaparece, ligera, arrebatada por la ola de un «Adiós», agudo y penúltimo, que me salpica todo el rostro de adioses menudos y acariciadores, como gotas.

Me quedo aquí, en la acera del bulevar, haciendo equilibrios sobre esta cuerda tendida sobre el vacío: «Un momento antes». Dos o tres transeúntes me tropiezan, están a punto de derribarme, creyendo sin duda que soy un hombre distraído, que estorba en medio de la acera, sin darse cuenta de que estoy entregado a una investigación delicadísima y desesperanzada: a averiguar qué cantidad de tiempo es ese que Livia me ofrece para la despedida, un momento. Evidentemente por sí, un momento no es nada o es todo; habrá que fijarse puntos de referencia, arranques para la solución. Saco el reloj: son las ocho. Claro está que antes de las doce no debo ir a la estación. Me quedan, pues, cuatro horas. Sin embargo, Livia dudó mucho . . . Y, además, la estación está lejos. De modo que sí, iré a las doce, aunque sea un poco temprano; pero para eso hay que salir de la ciudad a las once y media. (Descubro con sorpresa que las cuatro horas tienen ya media hora menos.) No sé si encontraré coches; tendré que ir a buscar uno al círculo. Y como el círculo está lejos de donde vivo, a veinte minutos, saldré de casa a las once. (Las cuatro horas se han reducido a tres.) Iré dando un rodeo, por la orilla del río, aunque tarde un poco más y tenga que anticipar la salida a las diez y media. Pero, en ese caso, sólo dispongo de poco más de dos horas para vestirme y cenar . . . Y me sorprendo de pronto con un silbido en la boca y el bastón en alto parando a un taxímetro que cruza. Lo raro, lo inexplicable, es que no doy al «chauffeur» las señas de casa, sino exactamente esta orden: «De prisa, a la estación del Este, al restaurán». Y, derribado en el coche, voy respirando voluptuosamente, no el perfume del jardín municipal, que atravesamos volando, sino el delicioso aroma de este razonamiento decisivo, casi narcótico: «Al fin y al cabo, lo mejor es eso: irse ya a cenar al restaurán de la estación. Así ya estoy allí, y luego no hay más que esperar un momento». Porque he decidido que el momento antes de la llegada del rápido de Praga empieza ahora, a las ocho y cinco.

«Acabo de llegar», contesto con aire indiferente a Livia, que me pregunta al presentarse en la gran sala de la estación, a la una y veinticinco, si me ha hecho esperar mucho. Ya trae puesta la cara de viaje, un rostro impersonal y anónimo a propósito para circular unas horas entre esas gentes compañeras y desconocidas que vayan en el tren, y ante las cuales no será, así, más que una pasajera que se reserva el vasto repertorio de sus gestos verdaderos para el punto de partida y el de llegada. Eso la confiere ya desde lejos un aire altivo e indiferente de reina, decorativamente corroborado porque se presenta a la cabeza de un séquito de esclavos, todos encorvados bajo el peso de tantos bultos, sus baúles, sus maletas, sus sombreras, y que defilan como en un friso, bajo su mirada faraónica, para ir formando en el suelo del andén una pirámide de objetos de viaje. Ahora Livia se inclina para buscar algo en un saquillo de mano, y no sé si es porque se colorean sus mejillas con el esfuerzo, o porque llevaba allí guardado su semblante íntimo y lo acaba de revestir para la despedida, ello es que me mira como me ha mirado siempre, como ya no me mirará (se va a marchar dentro de un instante) nunca. Y me dice:

«Ven, vamos a sentarnos en la sala de espera, tengo que hablarte.»

La sala, por un capricho exótico de la compañía, no del todo injustificado, pues la línea termina en Constantinopla, está decorada al modo oriental. Y sin duda, el ambiente es decisivo, hace creer a Livia que ésta de hoy es una de las mil y una noches, la impone un papel provisional y momentáneo de Scherazada, y la inspira, en vez de confidencias, de palabras últimas y definitivas, acaso de la revelación suprema que yo aguardaba, una historia inesperada, sorprendente, que escucho todo asombrado. Es la historia de una muchacha maravillosa. Tiene todas las perfecciones: una cultura hecha y deshecha, una belleza natural espléndida y superpuesta a ella otra hermosura elaborada y propia, todo el mundo visto y vivido detrás y otro mundo inminente, que ella va a inventar, ante sus veinticinco años. Como coquetería de su perfección un pequeño defecto, una miopía, sin la cual sería, inaccesible, extrahumana de puro perfecta. El entusiasmo con que habla de ella Livia (me dice que es su mejor amiga) es tan eficaz, tan activo, que la veo surgir poco a poco de la nada, modelarse, cobrar vida, y cuando Livia mete la mano en el bolso, no dudo que sea para extraer ya completa, lo único que falta, su persona misma, o cuando menos, en fotografía su efigie. Pero no es eso. Lo que Livia me muestra es un papelito azul, un telegrama donde leo: "Llegaré esta noche a la una y treinta y cinco. Susana». Porque su amiga se llama, aclara Livia, Susana. Yo, aunque inmóvil, quieto, en el diván miliunochesco, estoy en realidad haciendo esfuerzos desesperados, con las manos, con la razón, con la memoria, para desasirme de esta maraña en que me ha enredado Livia, perfidia final suya, que quiere dejarme así agarrotado, preso, en el enigma tejido con esos hilos de dos colores: Livia, Susana (Susana, el nombre de esta tarde, Livia, su mejor amiga . . . , inexplicable entonces que ella se vaya cuando la otra viene . . . Acaso . . .) Pero no; el embrollo aumenta prodigiosamente, me pierdo en él, renuncio a resolverle y pido a voces, en mi interior, un acero decisivo que corte, soltarlo es imposible, este enredo gordiano. Y como es la una y treinta y cinco, viene a tajarlo, afilado metálico y arrollador, la máquina del expreso de Praga, que entra, dominando su fuerza, como un atleta en un salón.

Nos acercamos. En una ventanilla se asoma una forma esbelta e inclinada de mujer, que al ver a Livia la tira presurosamente, como si tuviera miedo de que el tren siga corriendo y no pueda dársela, una sonrisa immensa y precipitada, tan densa, tan henchida, que al darme a mí, como me dio, en el pecho, porque a causa de la velocidad iba muy mal dirigida, me hace vacilar, me derriba casi, con un dolor nuevo en el corazón. Cuando me rehago veo que Livia y Susana, cogidas de la mano, sonrientes y fraternas, avanzan hacia mí, como desde el fondo de una mitología deconocida, ninfas liberadas del tren, dragón de hierro que tenía cautiva a una de ellas, y se adelantan en la iniciación de una ventura sin fronteras, la presentación de la nueva amiga. Pero, desgraciadamente, el mito nunca renuncia a una víctima, y el precio del rescate de ese alma que viene de París es ese cuerpo que se embarca apenas hecha la presentación ritual, sin tiempo para más, de un salto, en el tren de Praga. Y en ese salto de Livia, aparentemente libre y gozoso, al vagón, en esa entrega voluntaria y alegre al monstruo, veo, revelación final y cegadora, la ofrenda necesaria, el sacrificio ofrecido en aras de algo superior y perfecto, de algo que va a comenzar ahora. Porque, apenas el tren arranca, con un paso rítmico y sólido, como de frase de Sófocles, y me quedo solo con Susana en el andén, me doy cuenta de que el alma que hice para Livia, aquel alma profunda y perfecta, a mi imagen y semejanza, alma de mi amor, no la correspondía: es exactamente, sin una arruga, sin un defecto, la predestinada, la única para este cuerpo maravilloso que acaba de liberarse de ese cíclope con un ojo enorme y luminoso: el rápido de Praga, el rápido que se lleva en un lomo negro, en un silbido atronador, a mi Livia Schubert, definitivamente incompleta.